LOVE LEATHER ACCESSORIES

LOVE LEATHER ACCESSORIES

Zoe Larkins

20 easy leather accessories to sew

D&C
David and Charles

CONTENTS

INTRODUCTION

As a little girl, my first true loves were BA Baracas from the A-Team and Boy George, and I'm pretty certain that their styles influenced my love of accessories as I grew older. In more recent years, my style icons have become more colourful and feminine in the guises of Frida Kahlo and Carmen Miranda, who I'm sure you'd agree are both accessorized to the eyeballs – and that's the look I love!

In an age of mass production, I think it's so much more fun and far more original to make your own accessories. It's always such a great feeling when someone compliments you on something you've crafted and you can casually reply, 'Yeah, I rustled up this beaut with these nifty hands of mine.' You can wear the plainest outfit but make it look something really special if you have a scrummy, colourful necklace to jazz it up, or you can add a collection of snazzy brooches to pep up a simple top.

If you can't afford to buy a new outfit every month, this book provides you with a playful fashion accessory or two to stitch through the months of the year, from January to December. At the beginning of each project you'll see a list of what you'll need then I provide a step by step guide to make that month's accessory. All the project templates are at the back of the book, ready for you to copy; and my dear cat Jack makes an appearance every now and then with purrrrfect sewing tips for you, and other kitty cat comments. In addition, I have provided a list of materials and equipment at the front of the book, and all the techniques you will need are explained at the back.

Some projects are easier to make than others, but as long as you follow the instructions closely, in no time you will have a glorious array of scrumptious leather accessories. So if your pay packet doesn't leave you with much once the bills have been paid, these projects will hopefully inspire you to start accessorizing and customizing the contents of your wardrobe instead.

If you can fit in just one crafting session a month, I'm pretty certain that'll make you a much jollier person in general. Most of the projects should just take a couple of hours, and you don't have to sew alone. On a rainy day, invite a couple of chums round and make an afternoon of it. A Victoria sponge cake and a large pot of tea are compulsory, and I highly recommend making June's strawberry projects in the garden with a jug of Pimms and your favourite friends.

A LOVE OF LEATHER

My love of working with leather began while I was studying for my degree in silversmithing and goldsmithing (yeah, yeah, I chose the wrong course!), as I began to combine leather with metal. It was love at first stitch with leather, as I realized that this material doesn't fray, and has a special, snazzier quality than felt. The bold, jewel-like colours of the leather really had me going, and when I discovered you could buy metallic leathers… Well, that had me breathing into a brown paper bag! If you aren't keen on working with leather, PVC leatherette does the job just as well, or even good quality felt. So don't be concerned if you are of a vegetarian or vegan persuasion; there's a way around everything!

MATERIALS AND EQUIPMENT

On the following pages I will introduce you to the basic materials and equipment you will need to complete the projects in this book. If you're a keen crafter already, I'm sure you'll have some of the bits and bobs already in your possession, but if not don't worry, as none of the equipment will break the bank! Most items can be found in your local haberdashery store, or sometimes it's worth hunting about online if you want a bargain and are willing to wait a few days for delivery. For information on how to use many of these items, please see the Techniques section (see Techniques).

SOURCING YOUR LEATHER

There are all sorts of different leathers available, but the projects in this book are all made using nappa leather, which is super soft and supple, therefore easy to stitch by hand. One side is smooth leather, and the other is soft, fuzzy suede. When working through the projects take care not to mark the leather side, as this is what will be on show. The best thing about working with leather? It doesn't fray! But be aware that once a needle goes in, that hole is there to stay; this is why we glue leather, and don't use pins.

I source my leather from various wholesalers around East London's Brick Lane, where I can buy large skins of almost every colour under the sun. However these sorts of wholesalers tend to sell only large quantities, so if you are after a small amount you should be able to find traders who sell smaller pieces of leather and scraps at markets in larger towns and cities.

If you're unable to discover such a trader near you, simply look online at websites, such as Ebay and Etsy, to buy these smaller amounts; enter 'nappa leather' into your search engine and this should throw up some useful resources. Sometimes you can strike lucky and come across large batches of different coloured offcuts online to purchase relatively cheaply.

If you are a keen upcycler, you can always chop up a hideous 1980s blouson leather jacket and use that for your leather projects. Keep a sharp eye out at your local charity stores for leather fashions that totally missed out on style, but will nevertheless provide you with an excellent source of leather materials. In addition upholsterers sometimes have leather offcuts available, although they often use a thicker hide that can prove pretty hard work to sew by hand.

As you are looking to source your leather, please just bear in mind that the softer the leather is, the easier it will be to sew. And if you are buying larger quantities, leather comes in square foot measurements, not on a roll by the metre; it was an animal once!

As I mentioned in the Introduction, if you're not keen on the idea of using leather, PVC leatherette makes a fantastic cheaper alternative. It's super easy to sew - you don't even need to use a special leather needle - and unlike leather, you can buy it by the metre. Don't bother using the flimsy dressmaking PVC; instead source thicker material from upholstery stores or an online source.

LEATHER NEEDLE

Don't even attempt to sew leather without one! But treat with care, as a leather needle has a sharp triangular tip that really hurts if it slides under your fingernail. The brand of leather needle I use is called Whitecroft Essentials; I've tried others, but they just don't seem to cut the mustard! You can buy your own leather needles from all good haberdashery stores. It's worth keeping some novelty plasters (band aids) close to hand when using these needles; retro tattoo designs are my plasters of choice.

THREAD

Black and white are the main thread colours used for sewing the projects in this book, although you'll also need a little yellow and pink for the Fab lolly project.

I use topstitch thead, which is thick and strong, and usually used for sewing jeans and buttons. Gutermann Mara 30 is my personal favourite, but most brands make their own version, which you can purchase from good haberdashery stores. Of course you could use normal sewing thread, but this thick thread makes your work look more professional, and there's less chance of it breaking.

THIMBLE

I couldn't live without my thimble, to the point that I actually have a thimble tattooed on my wrist! A thimble is tricky to use at first, but once you develop a sore hole at the top of your finger from pushing a leather needle through leather without one, you'll take to it like a duck to water. Just make sure the thimble you purchase fits your finger perfectly;

a loose one that flies off at any opportunity is frustrating, and slows down your sewing.

SCISSORS

I have a large pair of sharp scissors to cut out the bigger pieces of leather rather than snipping away with a teeny pair of scissors, and these long blades tend to create a smoother edge. I also have a small pair of sharp scissors for cutting out fiddly little shapes, and for reaching the corners when trimming leather edges. Keep all your scissors away from paper, as using them to cut this will make them blunt.

LEATHER PUNCH

Invest in a good leather punch. You will need one with an adjustable head, which allows you to change the size of hole you wish to punch. This can be used on leather or paper, but resist the urge to make confetti as paper will make it blunt, and therefore difficult to punch clean holes in your leather. Cheaper punches may work well on thick leather, but soft nappa leather needs a good sharp punch. You can buy an adjustable leather punch in most haberdashery and DIY stores. When you go shopping for your leather punch, take a small scrap of nappa leather with you, bat your eyelashes then ask nicely if you can test it out before buying the punch, otherwise it's really quite annoying to find it doesn't cut through the leather when you get it home.

FINDINGS

Items such as brooch (pin) backs, earring hooks (wires), necklace chains, ring attachments, key rings, shoe clips, jump rings and headbands will always come in useful for your crafting projects, and we will use all of them in this book. You can buy most of these findings from good haberdashery and craft stores. Websites such as Ebay and Etsy are great places to source them at competitive prices, especially if you are looking to buy in bulk and happy to wait a few days for delivery. Just remember to check the measurements carefully before clicking the 'buy' button. Keep a stash of these goodies to hand, so you're always ready to craft a leather accessory at a moment's notice!

POPPERS (SNAP FASTERNERS)

Classic metal poppers (snap fasteners) come in handy when you want to make a simple fastening. I seem to have inherited hundreds of vintage poppers, neatly arranged on lovely cardboard packaging. These are stashed away in a glass jar, along with the rest of my findings.

BEADS

For some of the projects in this book we use seed beads. These are teeny-tiny beads that you can buy from all good haberdashery and craft stores. When you're trying to fit a needle through the holes of these beads the task can prove a little fiddly, particularly when it comes to sewing them onto leather using a leather needle. So although glass beads are nice, I tend to use the plastic variety, as they generally have a hole that is large enough to thread the needle through easily.

It's always handy to have a variety of coloured beads, large and small, hanging around, as they work well for replicating all sorts of things, from the beady eyes on a mouse to the centres of tiny forget-me-not flowers. For December's Mistletoe Kiss-mass necklace project we use larger 8mm ($3/8$in) diameter pearl beads, but as with seed beads, remember to double-check the size of the hole on these.

POM-POMS

Everyone loves a colourful pom-pom, don't they? And for January's project, I use them to brighten up a bobble hat and mitten brooch. You can buy packets of assorted colours and sizes for very little money in craft stores or individual pom-poms from haberdashery departments. Once I've picked out the ones I need for my sewing projects, I like stringing the rest of the packet contents onto thread and using them as simple yet snazzy garlands.

FLAT-NOSED PLIERS

You will need two pairs of these to open and close jump rings. Without them you will end up wrecking your fingernails, scissors, or anything else you try using instead!

WIRE CUTTERS

These are used to chop your necklace chains to the required length. As with the pliers, you can buy these from craft or DIY stores.

PHOTOCOPIER

You will need access to a photocopier so you can photocopy the templates prior to use, unless you really want to cut up this beautiful book! A photocopier will also prove handy for enlarging or shrinking templates, in case you feel like making a gigantic watermelon hairslide, or a teeny-weeny mouse necklace instead.

CARD

To create sturdy templates from your paper photocopies, use the card from old cereal boxes and the like.

PENS

Pens are used for drawing around templates onto leather before cutting out your shapes. A normal biro or felt-tip will be perfect for drawing onto lightly coloured leather. However it can be tricky drawing around a template on dark leather, so use a gold pen that will show up clearly.

MOUNTBOARD

When I first started working with leather, I used to glue layers of pizza boxes and cereal packets between the leather to stiffen my necklace designs. Then I discovered that mountboard does the job perfectly, and saves a whole lot of time and glue. You can pick up mountboard from artist's suppliers, or make friends with a picture framer who might let you have some offcuts.

GLUE

Any pva (white) glue or leathercraft cement will work for the leather crafts in this book, as long as it dries clear. Do make sure the bottle has a nozzle on the top, as this will really help when you are painting thin lines of glue onto your leather and mountboard surfaces. Glue sticks work just as well on larger areas that need securing, although these can prove a little difficult to manoeuvre when you just need a fine line around an edge. Don't settle for a cheap variety of glue stick, but choose a well-known brand such as Pritt Stick; it dries quickly, and sticks the leather down like no other glue I know.

POLYESTER STUFFING

You can buy bags of polyester stuffing that is used for filling soft toys from haberdashery and craft stores. If you love to upcycle, cut open an old cushion that's gone a bit flat then tease out the filling to make it as fluffy as candy floss, which works just as well.

THE PROJECTS

For every month of the year, there's a fun project to sew.... You'll find all the templates for each project at the back of the book, and if you fancy making June's project in October no one will tell you off! Once you've mastered the art of crafting this delicious bunch of accessories, take a look at some alternative designs I've provided to get your brain whirring with some other ideas for stitching.

YOU WILL NEED:

Red leather, 7 x 16cm (2¾ x 6¼in)

Pale blue leather, 1.5 x 6cm (⅝ x 2⅜in)

White thread

Brooch (pin) back

2 small blue pom-poms, 8mm (⅜in)
  diameter

Medium blue pom-pom, 2cm (¾in)
  diameter

Parcel string, 15cm (6in) length

Polyester stuffing

BOBBLE HAT AND MITTENS BROOCH

When it's frosty outside and you're suffering from the January blues, this cute little brooch will cheer up any winter outfit you choose to wear. So step out of hibernation and start stitching!

STEP 1.

Cut out the leather shapes using the templates provided (see Bobble hat and mittens templates). Stitch the brooch (pin) back onto the red hat-shaped back piece, then glue the pale blue strip of leather onto the red front piece to create the hat's trim **(A)**.

STEP 2.

With the white thread, sew a small, neat running stitch along the top of the blue strip, then 15 vertical stitches along the middle, to create a ribbed effect. You needn't worry about stitching around the edges of the blue trim at this point, as you will do this at the end. Using the same thread, stitch three snowflake shapes across the middle of the red front piece, making the middle snowflake larger than the two outer ones **(B)**.

STEP 3.

Take one pair of the red mitten shapes, ensuring they are opposites. With the white thread, stitch a snowflake in the middle then a ribbed cuff at the base of each mitten **(C)**. For the ribbed cuff five stitches should do it, much like you did on the hat.

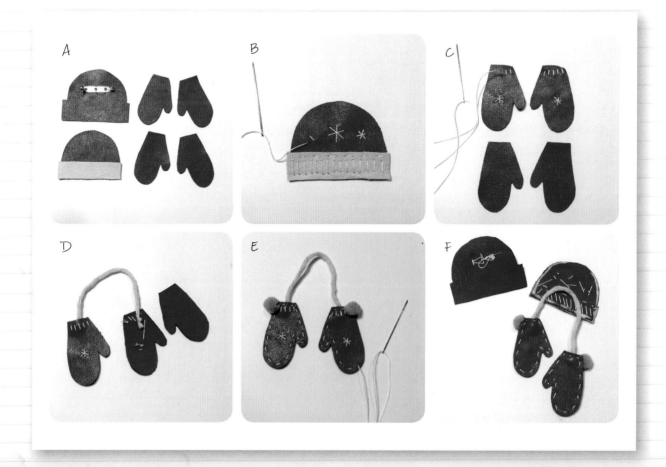

STEP 4.

Glue the backs of the red mittens into place, sandwiching one end of the string between the two layers of leather in the centre of the cuffs (D). It's a good idea to tie a small knot on each end of the string before you glue, so that it can't slip out once the mittens are stitched.

STEP 5.

Now sew a small, neat running stitch around the edge of each mitten, not forgetting to sew a tiny blue pom-pom on the edge of each one as you go (E). At the same time, make sure the string is securely stitched into the cuffs.

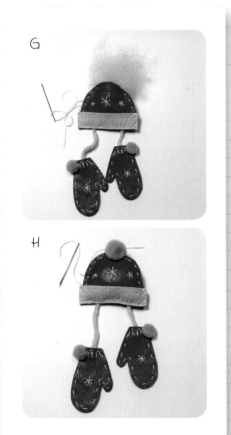

G

H

STEP 6.

Paint a thin line of glue around the very edge of the stitched bobble hat, leaving a finger-sized gap at the top (F). Make sure your mittens are facing the correct way, then glue the string to the suede side of the hat. I like it when the mittens hang at different levels, but you can glue them to hang where you like. Then stick down the back piece of the hat, so you have sandwiched the string in between.

STEP 7.

Trim off any excess leather around the edges of the hat then, starting at the gap, sew a small running stitch around the edge, securing the string as you go. Once you arrive at the other side of the gap, poke in small amounts of polyester stuffing until you are happy with the hat's plumpness (G).

STEP 8.

Carry on your running stitch to sew up the gap, not forgetting to add the larger bobble in the middle (H). Finish off your stitching, snip the thread - being careful not to snip your mittens off in the process - then pin the brooch onto your favourite winter coat.

YOU WILL NEED:

Red leather, 8 x 17cm (3¼ x 6¾in)

White leather, 2 x 4cm (¾ x 1½in)

Black leather, 4 x 6cm (1½ x 2⅜in)

Pale pink leather, 2 x 4cm (¾ x 1½in)

Black thread

Pair of shoe clips

Mountboard

Polyester stuffing

MR AND MRS LOVEHEART SHOE CLIPS

I just adore vintage Valentine's Day cards, particularly the kitsch and colourful imagery of 1950s designs. These shoe clips were inspired by one delightful illustration I discovered a while back, and, let's face it, who doesn't love a cute little face on a pair of shoes? These romantic lovelies will spruce up any pair of plain shoes for a special Valentine's Day date!

STEP 1.

Using the templates provided (see Mr and Mrs Loveheart templates), cut out four red hearts (two will be used for the reverse side), four white eye shapes, four black pupils, a dashing black moustache for Mr Loveheart, and two black sets of eyelashes, a pair of pink lips and a pair of pink cheeks for Mrs Loveheart. As you cut, don't forget to flip over the template for the opposite set of eyelashes!

STEP 2.

Glue the eyes, and the moustache or lips and cheeks, on each heart, as appropriate. With black thread, appliqué stitch every piece into place until they are all secure and there's no threat of a peeling eyelash or a loose moustache tip (A). Pop a tiny white stitch on each eye to give it a little twinkle!

STEP 3.

Your next job is to stitch the shoe clips onto the leather side of the spare red heart shapes (B). You need to position them in the heart centres, close to the top, leaving about a 5mm (¼in) gap between the top of the clip and the top of the heart. Don't forget to double-check which way the clips open up, as sewing them on upside down will prove disastrous when you try to clip them on your shoes at the end! You can go crazy with your stitches at this point, as you want to ensure these clips are super secure.

STEP 4.

Again using the template, draw two heart shapes onto the mountboard then cut them out approximately 5mm (¼in) inside the line, so they are slightly smaller than the original template.

A   B   C

D   E

JACK CAT SAYS

I like to wear these Loveheart clips on my paws when I'm in a particularly loving mood. Plus they soften the blow when I deliver a scratch...

Glue each mountboard heart onto the suede side of the hearts with the shoe clips stitched on the back. If you have positioned these mountboard hearts correctly, there will be a fairly equal amount of excess leather around the edge.

STEP 5.

Grab your glue and with a steady hand paint a thin line around the edge of excess leather left around each heart (C). Be sure to stay clear of getting glue on the mountboard - you just want this glue right on the edge of the leather. Whatever you do, don't forget to leave a small gap to poke in the stuffing at the end - one measuring about 2cm (¾in) should do it.

STEP 6.

Stick the heart faces onto each back. Once they are glued down, you may want to tidy up the edges with a quick trim.

STEP 7.

With a length of black thread, stitch around the edges of the hearts, starting at one end of the gap. Don't get carried away with your sewing and forget to pop the stuffing in when you reach the other side of the gap (D). I usually poke the stuffing in with the point of some small scissors, or a knitting needle - just be careful not to

stick this through your stitches by accident. Also, don't go too mad with the stuffing - your shoe clips want to be lightly padded, and the backs need to remain flat to sit correctly on your shoesies.

STEP 8.

Once the stuffing is in place, carefully stitch up the gap then secure your thread before snipping it off (E). When you've finished both Mr and Mrs Loveheart, you can clip 'em on your brogues, ballet pumps, or whatever you fancy. Now go and grab a date!

FEBRUARY

MR AND MRS LOVEHEART NECKLACE

This necklace snazzes up a plain neckline. Teamed with polka dots galore and a gigantic hair bow, it's a look that never fails to raise a smile.

STEPS 1 AND 2.

Follow steps 1 and 2 from the shoe clip instructions (see Mr and Mrs Loveheart shoe clips) but this time use the necklace templates (see Mr and Mrs Loveheart templates) to cut out two heart shapes and one joined heart shape, instead of the four basic hearts.

STEP 3.

Again using the joined heart template, cut out a slightly smaller version in mountboard then glue this centrally onto the suede side of the joined heart shape, leaving a gap around the edge (A).

A

B

C

JACK'S TOP TIP

For full-on lovestruck and twinkly eyes, glue teeny-tiny crystals onto the black pupils to add that extra bit of bling.

YOU WILL NEED:

Red leather, 8 x 17cm (3¼ x 6¾in)

White leather, 2 x 4cm (¾ x 1½in)

Black leather, 4 x 6cm (1½ x 2⅜in)

Pale pink leather, 2 x 4cm (¾ x 1½in)

Black thread

Necklace chain

4 jump rings

Mountboard

Polyester stuffing

STEP 4.

Glue the Mr and Mrs Loveheart together so they overlap each other, using the joined heart template as a guide for positioning. Then stitch into place (B).

STEPS 5 TO 8.

Now follow steps 5 to 8 from the shoe clip instructions (see Mr and Mrs Loveheart shoe clips). Remember to stitch a jump ring onto either side of the hearts as you are stitching around the edge from which to attach the necklace chain (C). And there you have a darling necklace to match your shoe clips!

YOU WILL NEED:

Yellow leather, 7 x 9cm (2¾ x 3½in)
Turquoise leather, 7 x 11cm (2¾ x 4¼in)
Black leather, 2 x 4cm (¾ x 1½in)
Pale blue leather, 4 x 6cm (1½ x 2⅜in)
Gold leather, 6 x 6cm (2⅜ x 2⅜in)
Green leather, 2 x 4cm (¾ x 1½in)
White leather, 3 x 4cm (1⅛ x 1½in)
White thread
Metal headband
Gold seed bead

BLUE TIT HEADBAND

I love to watch all the activity out on the bird feeder while I'm eating my Coco Pops in the morning, and blue tits are a firm favourite of mine, as their colours pretty much scream 'Spring is here!' This headband is the perfect hairwear to take you from spring into summer. With all the small pieces of leather it may look a bit daunting but I promise, once it's all stuck down the sewing is easy-peasy!

STEP 1.

First you need to cut out all ten pieces of leather, using the templates provided (see Blue tit templates). Then you can pop the turquoise bird-shaped piece to one side for the time being, as this is used later for the reverse.

STEP 2.

Glue all the shapes - apart from the turquoise back and legs - into place. I find it easiest to start by gluing the turquoise tail shape onto the yellow base, lining up the diagonal end with the wing. Now stick down the pale blue wing, layering the small green triangular shape on top. Next glue the white head, with the black 'U' shape on top and the small turquoise cap above. Using the turquoise bird-shaped backing piece as a guide, attach the beak so it peeks out from behind the bird's face.

STEP 3.

With the white thread, appliqué stitch each piece into place (A). I start sewing from the tail and work towards the head, but you can work whichever way you feel comfortable. Don't worry if a piece falls off before you stitch it down; just glue it back again and carry on. Sew on the gold seed bead for the bird's eye, popping a couple of stitches through the bead to ensure it won't fall off.

STEP 4.

Once the main body has been stitched, glue the little gold legs on from behind so they poke out from the bottom. Don't worry about stitching them yet, as you'll do this when you sew on the backing.

A   B

STEP 5.

Pop on your headband to decide where you want to position your blue tit. I think it looks best just on the side, facing inwards. Once you've made your mind up, glue the bird onto the band. You may find it slips about a bit, but once you've glued the turquoise bird-shaped back in place it should stay put. Now glue the backing on so that the suede side sticks to the back of the stitched bird.

STEP 6.

The backing will overhang the bird slightly, in order to cover the back of the beak. You can now carefully trim off the excess, but mind you don't snip the bird's legs off!

JACK CAT SAYS

Mmmmm, I love blue tits. Simply delicious!

STEP 7.

With white thread, overcast stitch around the edge of your bird (B). The beak can be fiddly so don't worry too much about stitching it - just pop a couple of stitches through. When you get to the legs you needn't stitch around their edges - again, just pop a stitch through the top of each so there's no fear of the leg dropping off at any point. Once you have stitched all the way around the bird, finish off neatly - and voila!

APRIL

YOU WILL NEED:

Blue leather, 9 x 10cm (3½ x 4in)

White leather, 5 x 6cm (2 x 2⅜in)

Yellow leather, 2 x 3cm (¾ x 1⅛in)

Tan leather, 2.5 x 4cm (1 x 1½in)

Beige leather, 4 x 4cm (1½ x 1½in)

White thread

Necklace chain

4 jump rings

Mountboard

Adjustable leather punch

DIPPY EGG NECKLACE

Everyone loves a dippy egg and soldiers, right? I know it was my favourite breakfast as a kid, and I'm still rather partial to a dippy egg even now! Team this necklace up with a jolly red gingham outfit and you'll look like a breakfast table at a seaside bed-and-breakfast - and that is no bad thing in my opinion....

STEP 1.

Cut out all of the leather shapes using the templates provided (see Dippy egg templates). Now glue the front pieces in place: the white stripes onto the blue egg cup shape, then the beige eggshell behind the egg cup so it is sticking up just behind the rim, with the egg white behind the shell and the yellow yolk piece on top, so it appears to run down the beige shell **(A)**.

STEP 2.

Once all the shapes are stuck in place appliqué stitch each piece down with white thread, making sure all the fiddly little pieces are well secured **(B)**.

STEP 3.

Using a pencil, draw around your dippy egg onto the mountboard. Taking the leather egg away, draw a smaller version inside this outline that is approximately 5mm (¼in) smaller all the way round. Then cut out the board shape **(C)**.

STEP 4.

Glue the mountboard egg shape onto the reverse of your leather egg then glue the blue leather back piece in place so that the board is sandwiched in between **(D)**.

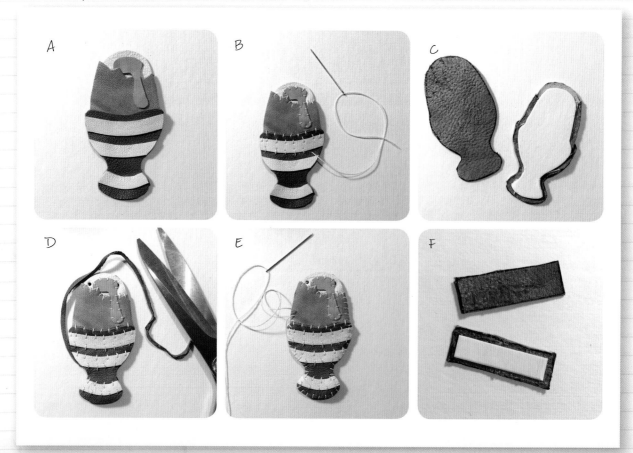

STEP 5.

Now is a good time to punch two small holes at the top of your egg through which to attach the jump rings. Once you have done this, trim off any excess leather from the edges then overcast stitch your way all around the entire egg **(E)**.

STEP 6.

Next, use the two tan rectangles - these are for your toasted soldier - to cut one slightly smaller version from the mountboard **(F)**. Glue the mountboard piece between the tan rectangles, making sure the leather is facing outwards.

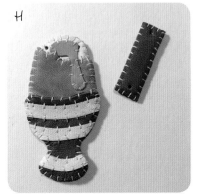

STEP 7.

Punch a small hole in each end of your tan soldier (G). Then use the white thread to overcast stitch around the outside of the soldier.

STEP 8.

Now both dippy egg and soldier are stitched (H), measure the length of chain you would like your egg to hang on. If your chain isn't ready made, pop a clasp and catch on it; otherwise go straight ahead and chop the chain in half to where you'd like your egg to hang. Use the jump rings to attach the egg to the chain, then decide where you want to position your soldier; I usually put mine about an inch or so away from the egg. Again chop into the chain then use two more jump rings to attach the soldier. Your delicious dippy egg necklace is now ready to wear!

JACK'S TOP TIP
You don't have to stick with a blue and white striped egg cup. Zoe sometimes likes to mix things up a bit, and makes them with white polka dots on a red background.

YOU WILL NEED:

Thick tan leather, 18 x 18cm (7 x 7in)

Pale pink leather, 9 x 9cm (3½ x 3½in)

Pale blue leather, 2 x 2cm (¾ x ¾in)

Green leather, 1 x 2cm (½ x ¾in)

White leather, 6 x 10cm (2⅜ x 4in)

White thread

2 black seed beads

Gold seed bead

Popper (snap fastener), 1cm (⅜in)
   diameter

BUNNY GADGET CASE

This beauty of a bunny will house your phone or iPod, and promises not to chew any wires or leave rabbit droppings around the place.

STEP 1.

Cut out the two case shapes in the thick tan leather, using the templates provided (see Bunny templates). The shorter tan shape is the front piece onto which you will stitch the bunny, while the taller tan one is the back piece. Also cut out the smallest curved shape from the pale pink nappa leather, which will act as a lining for the flap **(A)**.

STEP 2.

Now cut out the bunny shape, along with the ears, nose and flower details, using the templates provided (see Bunny templates). Then glue all these bunny shapes into place **(B)**.

STEP 3.

Using white thread, appliqué stitch all the pieces of the bunny face in place **(C)**. Add the two black seed beads for eyes, and the gold seed bead as the centre of the flower.

STEP 4.

Next take three lengths of white thread and tie them together in the middle for the whiskers. Trim these to the required length then glue them onto the reverse of the bunny face, so they peek out at the sides of the nose **(D)**.

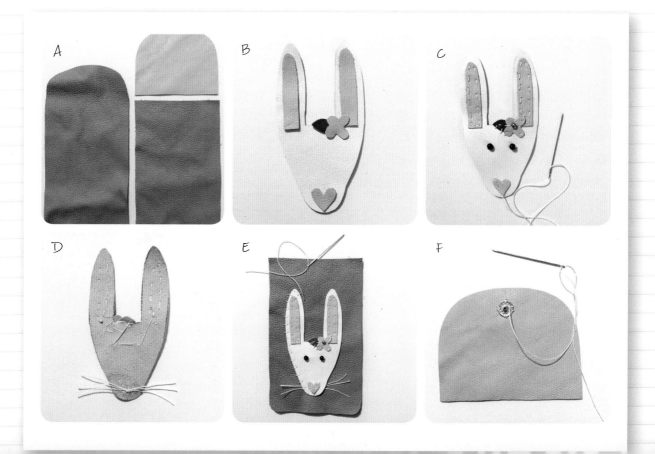

STEP 5.

Glue the bunny face onto the front piece of the case. Bear in mind that the flap will fasten at the top of this piece, so make sure the bunny is positioned fairly low down to accommodate this. Now appliqué stitch around the bunny face to keep it securely in place (E).

STEP 6.

Take the pink piece of curved leather for the flap lining. Fold this in half to find the centre, then stitch one half of your popper (snap fastener) in the centre, close to the curved edge (F). Three stitches through each popper hole should secure it sufficiently.

JACK'S TOP TIP

Rather than use the usual soft nappa leather for the case itself, Zoe uses a thicker leather from her local upholstery shop, as it's much more hardwearing. It is a little tougher to stitch through, so now is maybe the time to don a thimble!

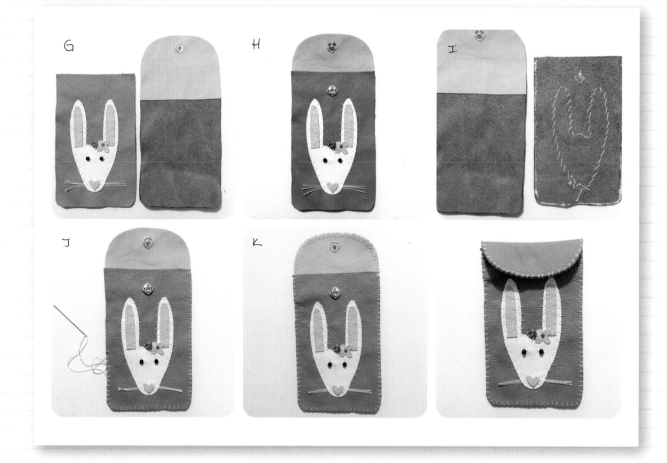

STEP 7.

Glue the pink curved piece, suede sides facing, to the tan back and trim if necessary **(G)**.

STEP 8.

Measure where your popper will fasten onto the front piece of the case then stitch on the other popper part **(H)**. You can check that it will fasten correctly by lining all the pieces up together and testing where the popper will lie.

STEP 9.

Glue a thin line around the edges of the front piece (I). Whatever you do, remember not to glue the top edge, as this is where your phone or iPod will fit in!

STEP 10.

Stick the back piece on, trim if necessary, then use the white thread to overcast stitch around the edge (J). I like to pop a couple of stitches through each side of the opening, as this is where the case will get the most wear.

STEP 11.

Stitch around the flap edge and, with any luck, once you are finished, the flap should fasten into place correctly (K).

JACK CAT SAYS

Phones tend to vary in size, so double-check the measurements of yours first. It's pretty simple to adjust the case shapes with the help of a trusty ruler!

MAY

YOU WILL NEED:

Grey leather, 9 x 16cm
  (3½ x 6¼in)
Pale pink leather, 4 x 6cm
  (1½ x 2⅜in)
White thread
2 black seed beads
Key ring
Polyester stuffing

MOUSE KEY RING

When I first moved to London, I lived in a teeny bedsit just off the Portobello Road. At night, when I was lying in bed, I'd often see a tiny little nose and set of whiskers poke out between the oven and fridge, which would sniff about. Then the sweetest little mouse would scurry out across the carpet. I loved that little fella, even if living with a wild rodent was totally gross and unhygienic. Anyway, this key ring is based on my furry London flatmate Marvin.

STEP 1.

Cut out the grey mouse shapes, using the templates provided (see Mouse templates). On one mouse shape, glue the two pink circles onto the ears and the small pink heart-shaped nose onto the face. Taking the pink strip of leather, pop some glue onto the end of the suede side. Then fold it in half lengthways, thread the key ring onto it and secure down the other end, so it creates a leather loop with the ring.

STEP 2.

With white thread, sew on the ears with running stitch, add two black seed beads for the eyes, then appliqué stitch the little pink nose in place **(A)**.

STEP 3.

Make a set of whiskers by tying three lengths of white thread together, trim to the required length, and glue behind the pointy nose. Paint a thin line of glue around the edge of the mouse, leaving a 2cm (¾in) gap on one straight edge to pop the stuffing in later, and glue the leather loop into place **(B)**. Then, suede side down, press the back mouse piece down onto the glued edges of the front piece.

STEP 4.

Trim the edges if necessary then overcast stitch around the edge of your mouse, starting at one side of the gap then working around **(C)**.

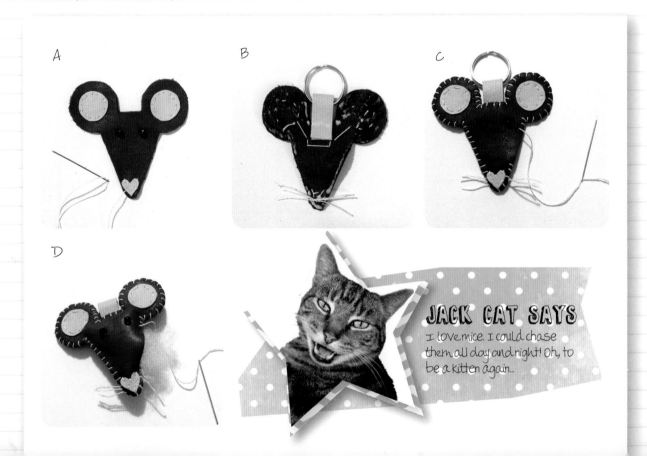

A

B

C

D

JACK CAT SAYS

I love mice. I could chase them all day and night! Oh, to be a kitten again...

STEP 5.

When you reach the other side, pause to poke in the stuffing (D). Push in a small amount at a time, to prevent any lumpiness.

STEP 6.

When you are happy with your mousie's plumpness, stitch up the gap and clip him onto your keys or handbag. This little guy promises not to leave droppings!

JUNE

YOU WILL NEED:

Red leather, 10 x 10cm (4 x 4in)

White leather, 2 x 2cm (3/4 x 3/4in)

Green leather, 6 x 10cm (2 3/8 x 4in)

White thread

Brooch (pin) back

Gold seed bead

Polyester stuffing

STRAWBERRY BROOCH

Strawberries may be a summer fruit, but I wear my fruity accessories all year round. There really is nothing more cheerful and fun than a plump, juicy strawberry hanging from your ear or lapel! At first these leather strawberries may seem a little tricky to make, but I guarantee that once you get the hang of it you'll be creating your own full crop of these beauts!

STEP 1.

Using the templates provided (see Strawberry templates), cut out two red leather semi circles, the green cross-shaped leaves, two sets of the large green leaves and the white flower.

STEP 2.

Now, one red semi circle at a time, paint a small line of glue down one half of the straight edge then fold over to create a leather cone, with the suede side facing inwards (A).

STEP 3.

With a needle and white thread, starting at the point of the cone, sew a small, neat running stitch along the join up to the top, then continue with your running stitch around the top edge of the cone.

STEP 4.

Once you have finished stitching around the top, you can start to gently pull the thread so the leather will ruche together. Before the hole becomes too small, carefully poke a small amount of stuffing in so this fills the point, then add more until it's looking suitably strawberry-like.

STEP 5.

Pull the thread tight to enclose the stuffing. Secure your strawberry with a couple of stitches across the top, making it as flat as possible.

STEP 6.

Now glue the green cross-shaped leaves to the top of your strawberry. Pop a small stitch in the tip of each green leaf to secure it, then again at the inner corners.

STEP 7.

Now for the fun part of creating your strawberry seeds! With tiny stitches and white thread, dot as many 'seeds' as you like all over the strawberry. You can push the needle right through to the other side, but try not to pull the thread too tight as you go, as this can make your

A

B

C

strawberry look a little bit mouldy
and dried out. Once you are happy with
the number of seeds you have stitched,
pull the needle out from the centre of the
leaves at the top then put to one side while
you make your other strawberry **(B)**.

STEP 8.

Stitch a brooch (pin) back onto the
leather side of one of the large green
leaf cut-outs. I tend to pop a couple of
stitches through each hole at the top and
bottom of the brooch to make sure it's secure.

STEP 9.

Take your two finished strawberries, and with the thread that you left hanging
from the tops, stitch each one onto the centre of the other leaf set. You want
your strawberries to dangle, so don't pull the thread too tight but make sure
they are secured well. Then stick the white flower over the top of where you
stitched the strawberries on. Grab the gold seed bead and stitch this onto the
middle of the flower.

STEP 10.

Now you can glue the leaf set
with the brooch back attached
onto the other leaf set, suede
sides together. Trim off the
excess to tidy.

STEP 11.

This part can be a little
tricky, what with the dangling
strawberries, but with a
little patience sew a neat
running stitch around the set
of leaves, and then through
the middle to represent
the leaf spine **(C)**. Your
brooch is now ready to pin
on your summer dress.

JUNE

YOU WILL NEED:

Red leather, 10 x 10cm (4 x 4in)

White leather, 2 x 2cm (¾ x ¾in)

Green leather, 6 x 10cm (2 3/8 x 4in)

White thread

Pair of earring hooks (wires)

Gold seed bead

Polyester stuffing

STRAWBERRY EARRINGS

The earrings are easy-peasy in comparison to the brooch. And you don't need to stop at just one strawberry per earring. Why not make a whole crop of strawberries to dangle from your ears? Tasty!

STEPS 1 TO 7.
Follow steps 1 to 7 from the brooch instructions (see Strawberry brooch).

STEP 8.
Using the piece of thread coming out from the top of the strawberries, now stich on your earring hooks (wires) **(A)**. It's as simple as that!

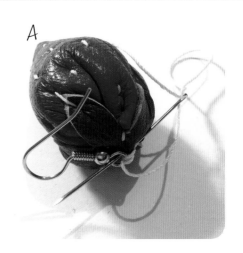

A

JACK CAT SAYS

I'd like a pair of these strawberries filled with catnip, purrrrrease!

JULY

YOU WILL NEED:

White leather, 4 x 7cm (1½ x 2¾in)

Dark brown leather, 2.5 x 4cm
 (1 x 1½in)

Bright pink leather, 2.5 x 4cm (1 x 1½in)

Cream leather, 1.5 x 4cm (⅝ x 1½in)

White thread

Pink thread

Yellow thread

Necklace chain

Jump ring

Mountboard

FAB LOLLY NECKLACE

I scream, you scream, we all scream for…Fab ice lollies,
please! It's July, and we should all be on the beach,
soaking up the rays, feasting on ice lollies. But on the
days where we have to do more boring things, like work
or study, this necklace will be a scrummy reminder of
days spent at the seaside.

STEP 1.

Cut out all the leather shapes, using the templates provided (see Fab lolly templates). Take the white rectangular shape and glue the dark brown shape at the top, the pink shape at the bottom, then tuck the cream lolly stick shape just behind the pink section. Punch a hole at the top centre of the brown part, as this is where you'll hang your lolly from the necklace chain.

STEP 2.

With white thread, appliqué stitch the pieces into place. Then use the same thread to stitch small lines in random directions on the brown section to represent sugar strands. Don't go overboard on the number of white stitches, but do the same with the yellow and pink thread to complete your sugar strands **(A)**.

STEP 3.

Now use the pink lolly-shaped template to cut out a smaller version of the same shape from the mountboard; one measuring approximately 5mm (¼in) less around the edge should be ideal **(B)**.

A

B

C

D

JACK CAT SAYS
You wouldn't catch me down the beach on a hot day. I prefer the cool shade under a bush in the garden.

STEP 4.

Glue the mountboard lolly shape onto the back of your stitched leather Fab (C). Then glue the pink version, suede side down, onto the other side, so the board is sandwiched between the two layers.

STEP 5.

Trim off any excess leather and re-punch your hole at the top, so this now passes right through the mountboard and pink leather back as well as the brown section. Overcast stitch all the way around your lolly and stick with white thread (D).

STEP 6.

Pop a jump ring through the hole at the top and then hang the lolly on your necklace chain to finish.

JULY

YOU WILL NEED:

White leather, 5 x 7cm (2 x 2¾in)

Dark brown leather, 1 x 3cm (⅜ x 1⅛in)

Yellow leather, 9 x 13cm (3½ x 5in)

White thread

Brooch (pin) back

Polyester stuffing

MR WHIPPY BROOCH

Someone once told me a trick to play with a Mr Whippy ice cream, which results in getting ice cream all over someone's face. I've never carried it out, not because I don't love a practical joke, but because I couldn't bear to waste delicious ice cream! In any case, this brooch looks great worn with nautical stripes for a super summery feel, while a seagull perched on your head will really complete the look!

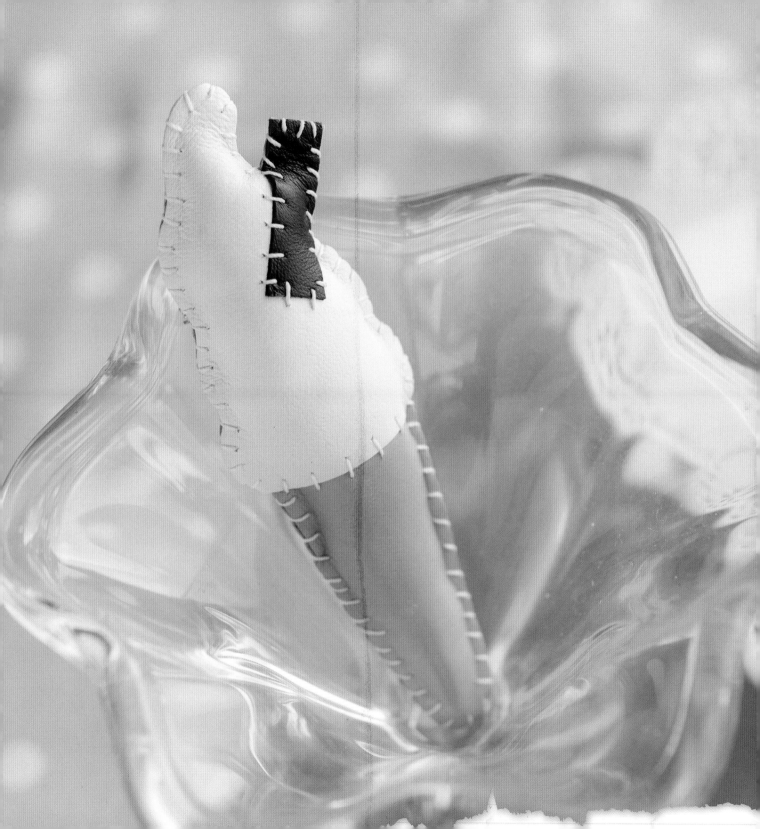

STEP 1.

Cut out the Mr Whippy shapes, using the templates provided (see Mr Whippy templates). Glue the white ice cream shape onto the top of the yellow cone shape, then glue the brown flake shape at an angle, using the yellow back piece to guide you where to position it **(A)**.

STEP 2.

With white thread, appliqué stitch the pieces into place where you have glued them. Then sew the brooch (pin) back onto the leather side of the yellow back piece **(B)**.

STEP 3.

On the back of your stitched Mr Whippy, carefully paint a very thin line of glue right around the very edge of the shape **(C)**. Just leave a 2cm (¾in) gap on one edge of the cone through which you will poke the stuffing later.

STEP 4.

Stick the yellow back piece onto the glue-edged Mr Whippy, suede sides facing. If you stitched your flake in the correct place, the shapes should line up perfectly. Trim off any excess leather once the glue has dried **(D)**.

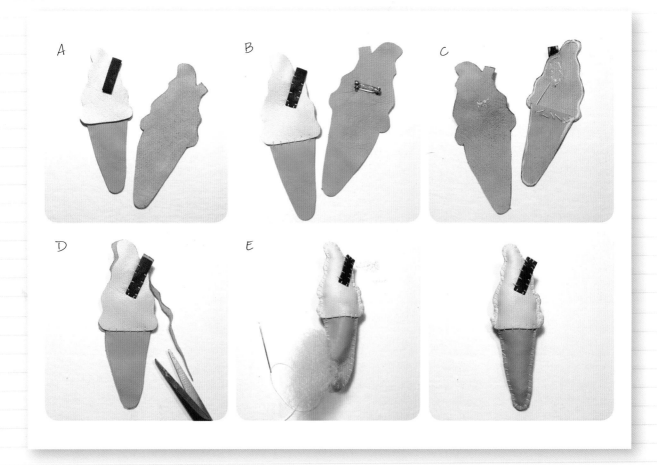

STEP 5.

Overcast stitch around the outside of your joined shapes, starting off at one side of the gap you left in step 3. When you reach the other side of the gap use a knitting needle to poke in the polyester stuffing, little by litte, until you are happy with the plumpness (E).

STEP 6.

To finish, sew up the gap. Your Mr Whippy brooch is now ready to adorn your beach bag, summer dress or grandma!

JACK CAT SAYS

I've never tried a Mr Whippy, but something tells me I'd like it...

WATERMELON NECKLACE

These juicy looking wonders work just as well whether you're festivaling in a field or holidaying in the tropics. The metallic pink and green colourway looks truly scrumptious together and with my favourite animal print on the reverse there's no reason why you couldn't wear them either way around.

STEP 1.

Using the templates provided (see Watermelon templates), cut out one pink watermelon slice and one leopard print slice, the slightly smaller slice-shaped piece in black, and the metallic green rind. Glue the green rind onto the curve of the pink slice.

STEP 2.

Grab your leather punch and use the smallest hole setting to punch a triangle of three holes into your pink slice. With tiny sharp scissors or a craft knife, fashion the holes with small points to look like seeds **(A)**. Once you are happy with these, glue the black leather behind the pink slice, leather way up, so the black leather is visible through the seed holes.

STEP 3.

With the white thread, now sew a line of running stitches along the edge of the green rind **(B)**.

STEP 4.

Cut a smaller version of the watermelon slice from the mountboard - one measuring 5mm (¼in) less all around will be perfect - and glue this onto the back of your pink leather watermelon slice **(C)**. Then cover the back with the leopard print piece, so the mountboard is sandwiched between.

STEP 5.

Trim the edges if necessary then punch a hole into the two corners of the metallic green rind. Overstitch around the edges of your watermelon and add the jump rings to the two corner holes. Finally, attach the necklace chain to the jump rings **(D)**, and there you have a spangly watermelon necklace!

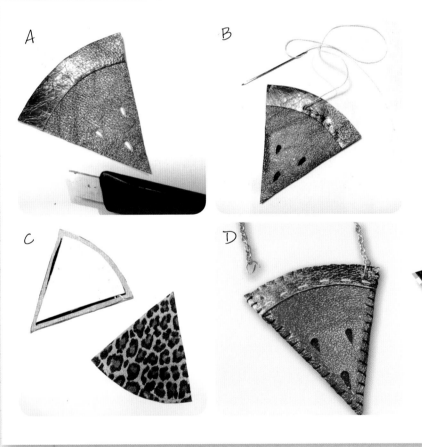

A

B

C

D

JACK'S TOP TIP

If you're not keen on sheeny-shiny metallics, non metallic colours will work just as well.

WATERMELON EARRINGS

Crimp your hair, pop on a cocktail dress and with these super duper earrings you are ready for some Club Tropicana fun!

STEPS 1 TO 5.

Follow steps 1 to 5 from the necklace instructions (see Watermelon necklace), but this time making two slices of watermelon.

STEP 6.

Instead of adding a necklace chain, attach a 3cm (2³⁄₈in) length of chain to each jump ring. Connect in the middle with another ring, which can then be attached to the earring hook (wire)**(A)**. Juicy earrings complete!

YOU WILL NEED:

Metallic pink leather, 6 x 11cm (2³⁄₈ x 4¹⁄₂in)

Metallic green leather, 7 x 14cm (2³⁄₄ x 5¹⁄₂in)

Black leather, 4 x 7cm (1¹⁄₂ x 2³⁄₄in)

Leopard print leather, 7 x 14cm (2³⁄₄ x 5¹⁄₂in)

Black thread

White thread

Pair of earring hooks (wires)

Gold chain, 6cm (2³⁄₈in) length

4 gold jump rings, 5mm (¹⁄₄in) diameter

Mountboard

Adjustable leather punch

A

JACK CAT SAYS

You wouldn't catch me wearing these earrings. For goodness sake, they'd get caught in the cat flap!

YOU WILL NEED:

Plain fabric, 42 x 24cm (16½ x 9½in)

Lining fabric, 42 x 24cm (16½ x 9½in)

Orange leather, 9 x 16cm (3½ x 6¼in)

White leather, 2 x 4cm (¾ x 1½in)

Pale blue leather, 2 x 4cm (¾ x 1½in)

Green leather, 2 x 4cm (¾ x 1½in)

Black thread

White thread

4 gold seed beads

2 black seed beads

Black satin ribbon, 2.5cm (1in) width,
 1m (40in) length

SQUIRREL COLLAR

On a recent walk through our town's gardens, we watched some super tame squirrels taking monkey nuts from a lady's hand. As squirrels scampered across the path, I noticed an unusal one. 'Oooh, look! That poor squirrel has lost it's bushy tail!' I exclaimed. 'That one's a RAT!' came the reply. Nevertheless, a cute squirrel collar is perfect for this time of year, when there's a chill in the air and you want to snazz up a plain oufit.

STEP 1.

Cut out the collar shape, using the template provided (see Squirrel templates). Fold your plain fabric in half widthways then pin the template onto it, making sure that the straight edge lines up with the fold in the fabric **(A)**.

STEP 2.

Cut out the collar. When you unpin the template and unfold the fabric, you should find that you have cut out a perfectly symmetrical Peter Pan collar shape, as shown **(B)**.

STEP 3.

Now use the templates (see Squirrel templates) to cut out from the leather two orange squirrels, along with the two blue and two white tiny flowers and four green leaves. Glue these into place on the collar as shown **(C)**, making sure they are not too close the edges by leaving a 1cm (½in) seam allowance all the way around.

STEP 4.

With white thread, appliqué stitch the squirrels onto the collar, adding a black bead to each one for an eye and gold beads for the centres of the flowers **(D)**.

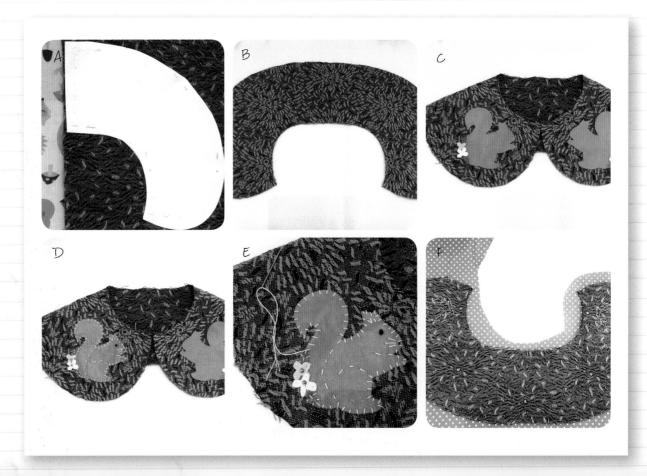

STEP 5.

Using the template as a guide, stitch the tail, leg, ears and whisker details on each squirrel. With black thread, stitch a tiny cross to create a nose on each (E).

STEP 6.

Lay the collar flat, right sides facing, on the lining fabric. Pin this into place then cut carefully around the edge (F).

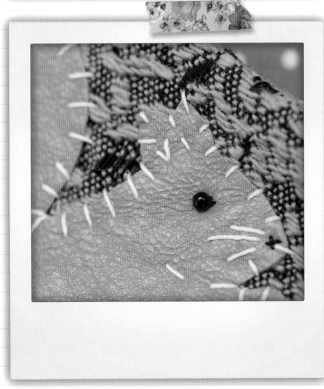

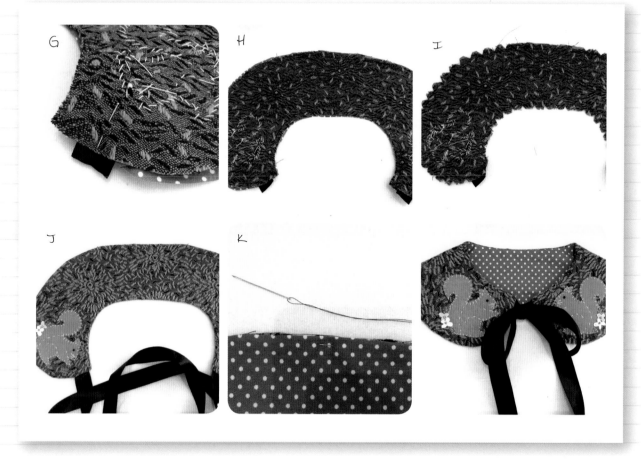

STEP 7.

Cut your length of black ribbon in half with a diagonal snip to prevent fraying. Insert one end of each piece between the collar and lining layers, so just a short straight edge of the ribbon protrudes slightly from each end (G). You might like to roll up the ribbon inside and secure it with a pin, so it doesn't get in the way when you sew the collar.

STEP 8.

With a sewing machine set to straight stitch, sew around the edge of the collar with a 1cm (½in) seam, leaving a 10cm (4in) gap on the top straight edge so you can turn the collar the right way around (H).

STEP 9.

With sharp scissors, cut notches all the way around the edge of the collar, taking care not to snip through your stitches (I). These notches will allow the collar to lay flat once you have turned it inside out.

STEP 10.

Turn the collar inside out then iron flat. Avoid ironing the leather squirrels, as sometimes the heat can cause the leather to shrink. Press the seams of the gap so they lie flat inside then pin these in place (J).

STEP 11.

With neat little stitches, hand sew the gap closed (K). Hoorah! Your collar is now ready to wear!

JACK CAT SAYS
Zoe used a fairly thick vintage fabric for this collar, with a light polka-dot cotton lining. You can use any fabric you like, but iron on some interfacing if the one you choose is lightweight or likely to fray easily. By all means go for a patterned lining, but stick with something plain for the outer garment so that your lovely squirrels stand out.

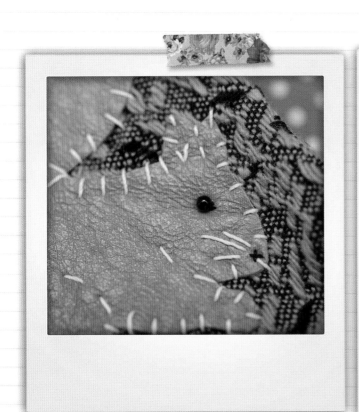

SEPTEMBER

YOU WILL NEED:

Green metallic leather, 8 x 10cm (3¼ x 4in)

Gold leather, 3.5 x 4cm (1³⁄₈ x 1½in)

Dark brown leather, 4 x 4cm (1½ x 1½in)

White thread

Gold necklace chain

Gold jump ring

Polyester stuffing

Adjustable leather punch

SUPER SHINY ACORN NECKLACE

There's nothing more pleasing to the eye than a juicy metallic leather, and this lovely shiny necklace is a definite eye-catcher. Just keep it outta sight of those greedy squirrels on woodland walks!

STEP 1.

Using the template provided (see Super shiny acorn templates), cut out one green oak leaf shape. Glue this onto another piece of green leather, suede sides facing, then trim around the edge so you are left with a double-sided metallic green oak leaf (A).

STEP 2.

Now cut out two gold acorns and two brown acorn cups from the templates (see Super shiny acorn necklace templates). Glue the acorns just behind the top edge of the brown cups then appliqué stitch along this join with white thread (B).

STEP 3.

Turn your stitched acorns over, so their suede sides are facing upwards. Paint a thin line of glue around the edge of one, leaving a 2cm (¾in) gap on one side (C), then stick the other acorn down onto it. They should fit together perfectly, but feel free to trim any excess leather if there is a little overlap.

STEP 4.

With the adjustable leather punch, make a small hole through the acorn and leaf stalks to accommodate a jump ring later (D).

STEP 5.

Now sew a running stitch line through the middle and around the edge of the oak leaf to create a leaf vein (E).

STEP 6.

Overcast stitch around the outside of your acorn, starting at one side of the gap. When you reach the other side, poke in some stuffing to achieve a nice plumpness (F).

STEP 7.

Sew up the gap, then attach both the acorn and oak leaf to the necklace chain using the jump ring.

JACK CAT SAYS

Take care not to over stuff your acorns, as sometimes the metallic leather can crack slightly if pushed too far!

OCTOBER

YOU WILL NEED:

Red leather, 7 x 11cm (2¾ x 4¼in)

White leather, 4 x 5cm (1½ x 2in)

Black leather, 1 x 1cm (⅜ x ⅜in)

Black thread

White thread

Key ring

Pearl seed beads

2 black seed beads

Polyester stuffing

TOADSTOOL KEY RING

Don your wellies and go for a traipse around the forest through the autumnal leaves, and if you're lucky you'll spot one of these super colourful, fairy tale-like toadstools. But if you can't get yourself out of the house, you can just make a cheerful toadstool fella to attach to your keys instead.... He's a super fun guy (sorry, just couldn't resist!).

STEP 1.

Cut out the toadstool shapes in leather, using the templates provided (see Toadstool templates). Using the red back piece as a guide, glue the white leather stalk to the red leather cap. With the black thread, sew on two black beads as eyes. Glue the small black semi-circular mouth shape in place on the white stalk then appliqué stitch this down, also with black thread **(A)**.

STEP 2.

Now with white thread, add as many pearl beads to the cap as you like, until it's looking suitably toadstool-y **(B)**. Also appliqué stitch the red cap to the stalk.

STEP 3.

Taking the white strip of leather, apply glue to one end of the suede then fold it in half lengthways. Thread the key ring onto it then stick the ends together to create a ring attached to a leather loop.

STEP 4.

Glue the end of the loop onto the top suede edge of the stitched toadstool. Paint a thin line of glue around the edge of the toadstool, leaving a gap of 2cm (1in) at the top **(C)**. Then stick the red back piece, suede side down, onto your toadstool.

STEP 5.

Trim off any excess leather from
around the edge (D). Then use the
white thread to overcast stitch
around the edge of the toadstool,
starting at one side of the gap (E).

STEP 6.

When you reach the other side poke
in the stuffing, a little at a time,
until you are happy with the plumpness
of your toadstool (F). Then to finish,
sew up the gap.

JACK'S TOP TIP

You could always glue on googly
eyes for a more comic effect.
Who doesn't love a pair of
googly eyes?

TOADSTOOL RING

A

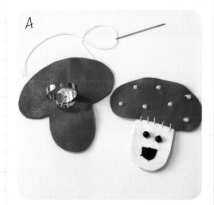

B

This slightly ridiculous toadstool ring will raise a smile from the gloomiest goblin in the forest! It's big, it's fun, it's colourful, it's got a smiley face... What's not to like?

STEPS 1 TO 2.

Follow steps 1 to 2 from the key ring instructions (see Toadstool key ring).

STEP 3.

With white thread, stitch your ring attachment onto the leather side of the red back piece **(A)**.

STEP 4.

Paint a thin line of glue around the edge of the toadstool, leaving a gap of 2cm (1¾in) at the top **(B)**. Then stick the red back piece, suede side down, onto your toadstool.

STEP 5.

Finish your toadstool ring by following step 5 from the key ring instructions (see Toadstool key ring).

YOU WILL NEED:

Red leather, 7 x 11cm
(2¾ x 4¼in)
White leather, 4 x 5cm
(1½ x 2in)
Black leather, 1 x 1cm
(⅜ x ⅜in)
Black thread
White thread
Ring attachment
Pearl seed beads
2 black seed beads
Polyester stuffing

NOVEMBER

YOU WILL NEED:

Brown leather, 12 x 12cm (4¾ x 4¾in)
Red leather, 4 x 5cm (1½ x 2in)
White leather, 2 x 4cm (¾ x 1½in)
Gold leather, 4 x 6cm (1½ x 2⅜in)
White thread
Brooch (pin) back
Black seed bead
Polyester stuffing

ROCKIN' ROBIN BROOCH

There's nothing that says 'Christmas is nearly here!'
more than a cheeky rockin' robin brooch pinned onto
your festive Fairisle knit!

STEP 1.

Using the templates provided (see Rockin' robin templates), cut out all the robin pieces and glue them into place. I find it easiest to line up and glue the white belly to follow the wing line first, then the red breast. You may find that the red breast overhangs slightly, in which case be brave and trim it down. Sew the brooch (pin) back onto the larger brown robin shape **(A)**.

STEP 2.

Glue the gold beak and legs onto the back of the robin, so when you turn it over the gold shapes peek out **(B)**.

STEP 3.

With white thread, appliqué stitch all the pieces into place. Use the template to guide you on where the stitched wing detail should go. Also, stitch in place a black bead for the eye **(C)**.

STEP 4.

Glue a thin line around the suede side of your stitched robin, leaving a 2cm (¾in) gap along the top straight edge into which you will later poke the stuffing **(D)**. Glue the back piece onto this, suede sides facing.

STEP 5.

Carefully trim off any excess leather from the edge (E), taking care not to snip off your robin's dainty legs!

STEP 6.

With white thread, start overcast stitching at one end of the gap and work all the way around to the other side (F).

STEP 7.

Now poke stuffing into the tail of your robin, little by little, with a pencil or knitting needle, then gradually fill the rest of your bird until you are happy with his plumpness (G). To finish, stitch up the gap, then pin him on your jumper and start feeling festive!

G

JACK CAT SAYS

I suggest you invite a bunch of friends over, crack open a bottle of sherry, feast on some mince pies, and start stitching a flock of robins together to kick start the festive cheer on a dark winter's night.

NOVEMBER

YOU WILL NEED:

Pair of gloves or mittens
Brown leather, 8 x 20cm (3¼ x 8in)
Red leather, 4 x 5cm (1½ x 2in)
White leather, 2 x 4cm (¾ x 1½in)
Gold leather, 4 x 6cm (1½ x 2⅜in)
Metallic blue leather, 3 x 7cm (1⅛ x 2¾in)
White thread
Black seed bead

ROCKIN' ROBIN CUSTOMIZED GLOVES

I love a good soft pair of leather gloves, but rarely do they come with a jolly design in place. Here's your opportunity to snazz-ify the boring gloves Auntie Ethel gave you last Christmas, which you stashed away in the back of a cupboard.... This design would look even cuter on a pair of woolly mittens, if you're not so keen on wearing leather gloves.

STEPS 1 TO 3.

Cut, glue and stitch the robin pieces together by following steps 1 to 3 of the brooch project (see Rockin' robin brooch). However, this time you don't need to cut out and work with the back piece; instead cut out the brown circle for the nest and three metallic blue egg shapes (see Rockin' robin templates), as shown (A).

STEP 4.

Glue the eggs in position on the nest then stitch them in place. Now use white thread to make random stitches around the eggs for a twig-like effect (B).

JACK'S TOP TIP

Steer away from dark black or brown gloves, as you want the robin and his nest to stand out against the background.

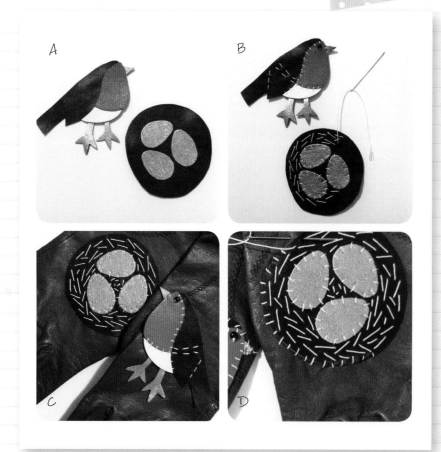

A

B

C

D

STEP 5.

Glue the robin onto one glove
and the nest on the other **(C)**.
I think it looks best if the
robin is facing the nest, so
bear this in mind when you are
positioning them.

STEP 6.

Appliqué stitch your robin and
nest onto the gloves **(D)**. This
part can be a little tricky,
so sometimes I pop a piece of
mountboard into each glove to
prevent me from stitching all
the way through to the glove
backs. This part does require a
little patience, but the result
is well worth it!

DECEMBER

CHRISTMAS PUDDING EARRINGS

I'm fairly certain that the best thing about Christmas is eating all the delicious food that you don't get to eat during the rest of the year; Christmas pudding being one of my favourite treats with scrummy brandy butter! These festive earrings will jolly up your ears on the run up to Christmas, and I always find these three-dimensional projects very satisfying to make.

YOU WILL NEED:

Dark brown leather, 7 x 14cm (2¾ x 5½in)

White leather, 4 x 8cm (1½ x 3¼in)

Metallic green leather, 2 x 4cm (¾ x 1½in)

White thread

Pair of earring hooks (wires)

6 red seed beads

Polyester stuffing

STEP 1.

Using the templates provided (see Christmas pudding templates), cut out two dark brown leather circles, two white icing splodges and four metallic green leaves. With white thread, sew a small running stitch around the edge of one dark brown leather circle (A).

STEP 2.

Gently pull the thread tight on the circle, so that the leather pulls together. Then, while you still have a gap at the top, push small amounts of the stuffing in (B). Do this bit by bit, until you feel your pudding is plump enough, but not so plump that you can't pull the thread tight in the next step.

STEP 3.

Now pull your thread tight to close the pudding then sew across the gathered area to secure it (C).

STEP 4.

Glue a white leather splodge shape over the top of the pudding then use small stitches to sew this in place (D).

STEP 5.

When you have finished stitching on the splodge, pull the needle out of the top middle part of the pud, glue on the two metallic green holly leaves then use tiny stitches to sew these in place (E).

G

STEP 6.

Once you have sewn on the leaves, add three red beads for berries between them **(F)**.

STEP 7.

Grab an earring hook (wire), and stitch this onto the top of your Christmas pudding **(G)**. Now you have one Christmas pudding earring you can wear it like a festive pirate. Or now you know how, start stitching the other one so you can wear a pair!

JACK CATS SAYS

If you have a furry feline friend like me, make them a catnip-filled felt pud as a Christmas treat. You can easily enlarge the templates to do this on a photocopier.

MISTLETOE KISS-MAS NECKLACE

Christmas just isn't Christmas without a snog under the mistletoe! This cute necklace will ensure you'll have a Merry Kiss-mas, and it's super easy to make.

STEP 1.

Cut out a mistletoe shape, using the template provided (see Mistletoe Kiss-mass templates). Then glue this, suede sides facing, onto another piece of metallic green leather and trim around the edge (A). Punch a small hole at the top of the stem.

STEP 2.

With the white thread, sew a small, neat running stitch around the edge of your mistletoe, stopping in the middle to sew on the three pearl beads (B).

STEP 3.

Carry on with the running stitch until you meet the other end, and finish off neatly (C). Pop a jump ring through the hole at the top, and thread this onto your necklace chain. Snogs ahoy!

JACK CAT SAYS
I don't do kisses, I do bites...
I like to call them 'love bites'.

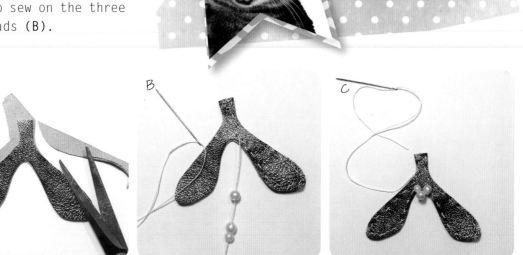

YOU WILL NEED:

Metallic green leather,
  7 x 15cm (2¾ x 6in)

White thread

Necklace chain

Jump ring

3 pearl beads, 8mm (⅜in)
  diameter

Adjustable leather
  punch

CUSTOMIZED PROJECTS

Once you have sussed out how to do the projects, you can become super creative and go offroad by mixing them up, as the examples on the following pages demonstrate. For instance, use the bunny designs from the gadget case, and pop 'em on some gloves instead. Create the perfect Christmas slipper by stitching some mistletoe on your pumps; we call these 'Mistle-toes'; clever, huh? Or snazz up some summer pumps with metallic watermelons. The blue tits can be turned into brooches, necklaces or key rings. Or with the help of a photocopier, shrink down the acorn template to make some dinky earrings fit for a squirrel. Enlarge the dippy egg template, and make a giant jolly breakfast brooch! And if you've gone a bit mad on making strawberries, attach them all to some cord, and you've got yourself a scrumptious necklace. The possibilities here are endless...

BUNNY
GLOVES

Seriously cute gloves for a rabbit lover...
You don't have to stick with leather
gloves, as you could always experiment
with knitted mittens instead.

MISTLETOE SHOES

The perfect shoes for sherry-sipping Christmas festivities. Plus you get to ask people to kiss your feet!

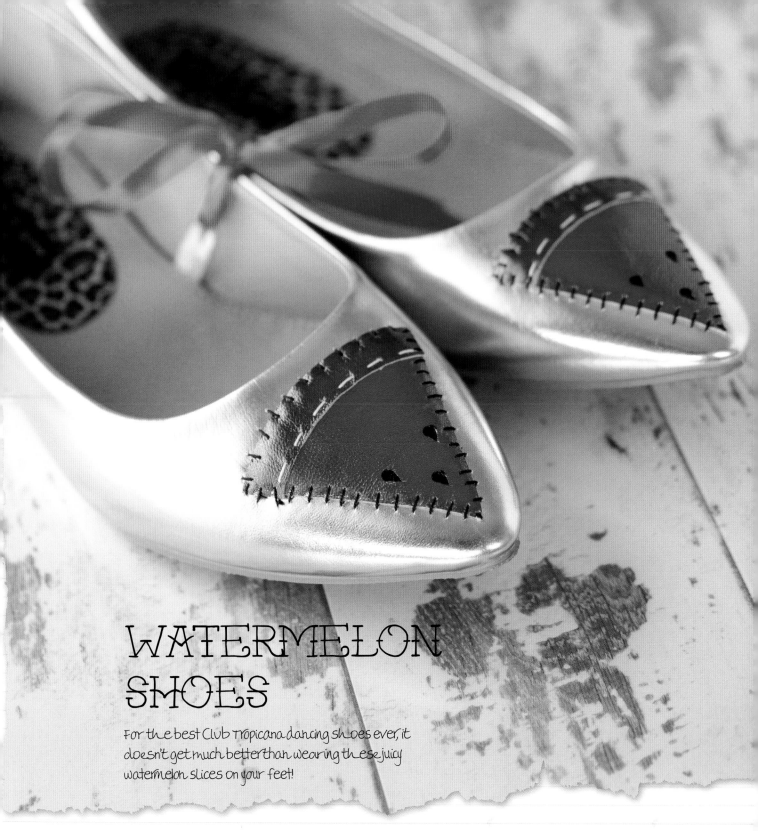

WATERMELON SHOES

For the best Club Tropicana dancing shoes ever, it doesn't get much better than wearing these juicy watermelon slices on your feet!

BLUE TIT BROOCH

Make a pair of these to face each other, pin them on your top, and wait for keen bird-spotters to comment on your lovely birds!

DIPPY EGG BROOCH

A massive dippy egg brooch on your cardi will always make you feel jolly! Try experimenting with different colours and jazzy patterns on the egg cup.

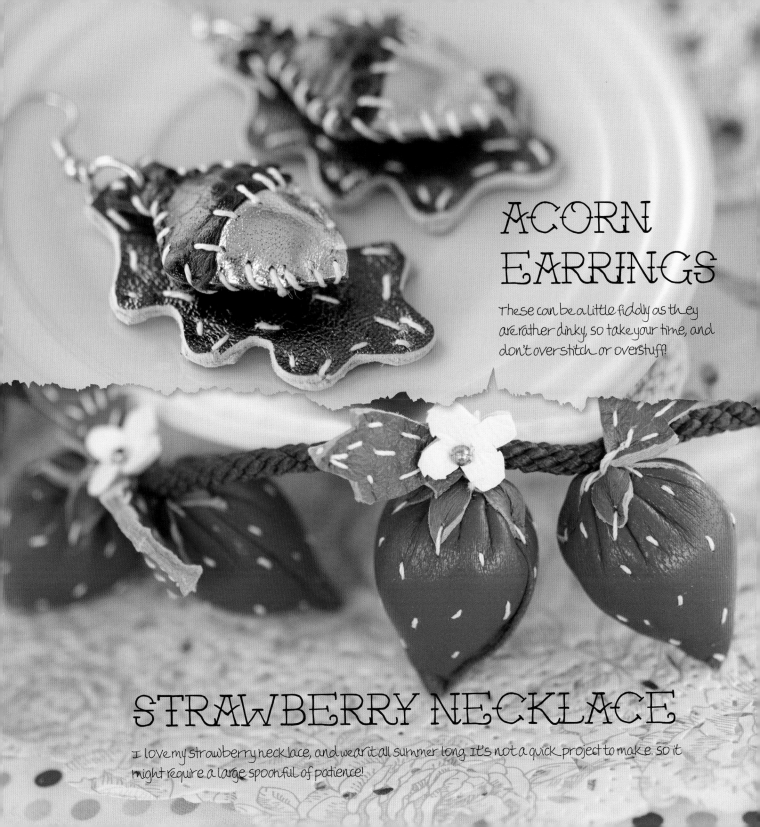

ACORN EARRINGS

These can be a little fiddly as they are rather dinky, so take your time, and don't overstitch or overstuff!

STRAWBERRY NECKLACE

I love my strawberry necklace, and wear it all summer long. It's not a quick project to make, so it might require a large spoonful of patience!

MR WHIPPY HAIRSLIDE

Try not to overstuff your Mr Whippy hairslide, as it looks better if it sits flat against your head. If you are in a rush, don't bother stuffing it at all and leave it flat.

ROBIN COLLAR

Choose a lovely vintage tweed for this festive collar. I have been known to cut up old moth-eaten skirts to make cutesie collars in the past just cover the holes up with your leather designs.

TECHNIQUES

This is the bit where I explain how to do stuff... So if you're wondering how to sew a certain stitch, this is where you'll find the explanation. I've tried to think of all the questions your brain could come up with in regards to the projects in this book, and have answered them all right here.

HOW MUCH THREAD DO I NEED?

There's a lovely German saying that translates into English as 'Long thread, lazy girl'. You might think a long thread will save you time by having to re-thread less frequently, but in fact a long piece of thread will slow down your sewing. It will easily become knotted, and will make you feel very cross, as if you'd like to throw your sewing across the room. Go for a shorter length; measuring a length from your hand to your elbow is a pretty good guide. If you run out halfway through a job, re-threading is far less annoying than becoming tangled!

HOW DO I START SEWING?

To get started, simply tie a knot at the end of your thread then push the needle up through the leather, so the knot is hidden on the reverse suede side **(A)**. When you are sewing around the outside edges of a project, start by sandwiching the knot between the front and back layer so it is neatly hidden away **(B)**.

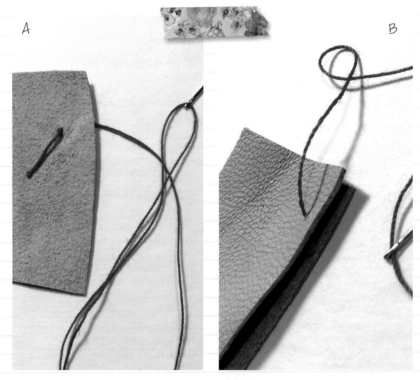

A

B

HOW DO I SEW A RUNNING STITCH?

Running stitch is the most basic of needlework stitches. Thread your needle and tie a knot at the end. Then weave the thread through the leather in an under-and-over action to produce a line of small, even stitches that together resemble a dashed line (C).

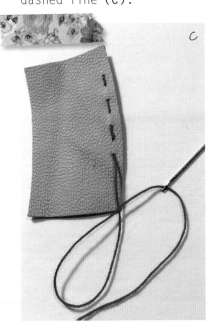

C

HOW DO I SEW AN APPLIQUÉ STITCH?

Appliqué stitch is a way of sewing shapes onto a background, creating a folk art look. Start by threading your needle and tying a knot at the end of your thread. Push the needle up through the underside of the leather, then down through the shape that is adhered to the surface. Keep stitching along the edge, until it is all securely tacked down (D). As a tip, it is easier to work by passing your needle up through one layer of leather, then pushing down through multiple layers. Try to keep the space between your stitches even so the result looks neat and tidy, although the odd rogue stitch you make will just add to the handmade charm!

D

HOW DO I SEW AN OVERCAST STITCH?

Overcast stitch is used to sew around the sides of leather shapes, attaching the two layers firmly together so they don't fray. Sew a line of neat, equally-spaced slanted stitches that loop around the edges of the leather (E). It can be tricky to make the stitches look straight, but by using your needle at an angle and with a little practise this will become achievable. Don't worry if your stitches appear slanted on the reverse, as no one will see those!

E

HOW DO I FINISH OFF MY SEWING?

Finishing off your sewing can seem a little tricksy, so here's how you do it. If you are finishing off an appliqué, pull your needle through to the back of the leather then push it back halfway so your needle doesn't come through the front. Do this a couple more times in the same spot until you are happy that your stitching won't unravel (A), then snip off your thread to complete.

To finish off an edge, use a similar technique. With your needle and thread pulled through to the reverse, stitch halfway through the leather a couple of times (B), so you end up with a chunky-looking stitch on the back and a normal stitch on the front, then snip your thread.

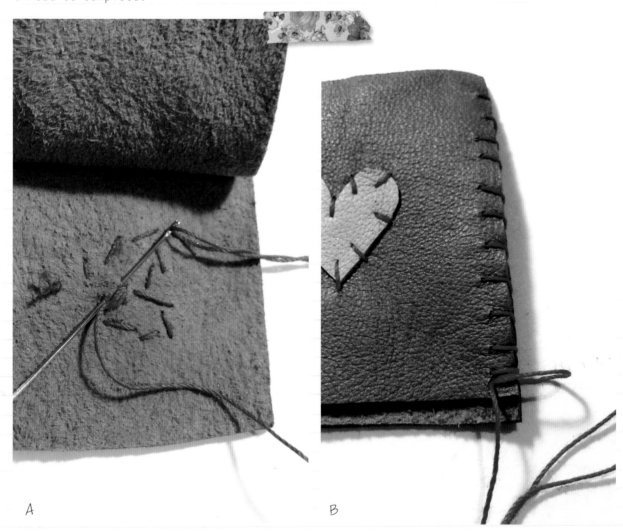

A

B

HOW DO I SEW BEADS ONTO MY LEATHER?

First, you need to make sure your needle will fit through the bead's hole. Once you have checked this, position your bead on the leather and stitch through the bead two or three times until you feel it is fully secure, then finish off **(C)**. If you have more than one bead to sew on no more than 1cm (½in) away, don't worry about tying off your thread and starting again; on the reverse, simply jump your needle and thread over to sew on the next one **(D)**. Just don't pull your thread too tight or the fabric will pucker; nice and loose is where it's at!

C

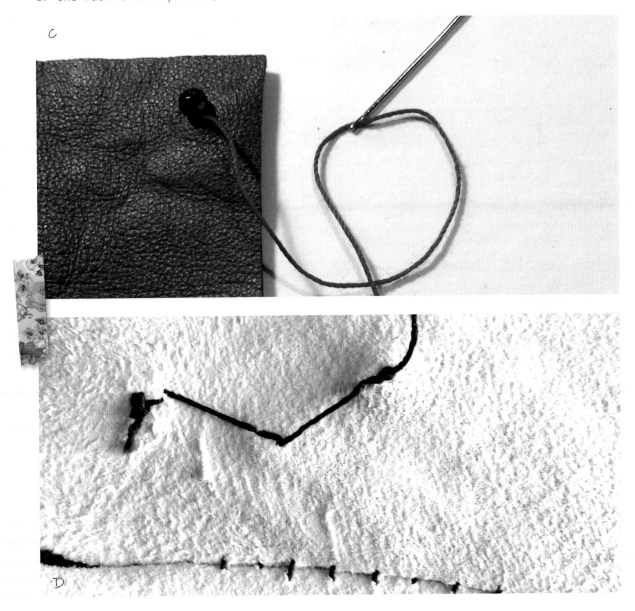

D

HOW DO I ATTACH FINDINGS TO MY LEATHER?

The key thing to bear in mind when stitching findings onto your leather is to make sure that they are secure and unlikely to fall off at the drop of a hat. It's good to make the stitches as neat as possible, but it won't be the end of the world if there is a rogue stitch or two; findings are usually fixed to the back of the accessory, so nobody is going see it once it's attached to you. And anyway, practise always makes perfect!

Brooch backs: Starting off with a knot at the back, stitch through each hole of the brooch back at least twice at both the top and bottom.

Shoe clips: With these, stitch through any holes you can. They can be quite stiff to clip on and off, so you need to make sure your thread won't unravel so your clips disappear down a drain!

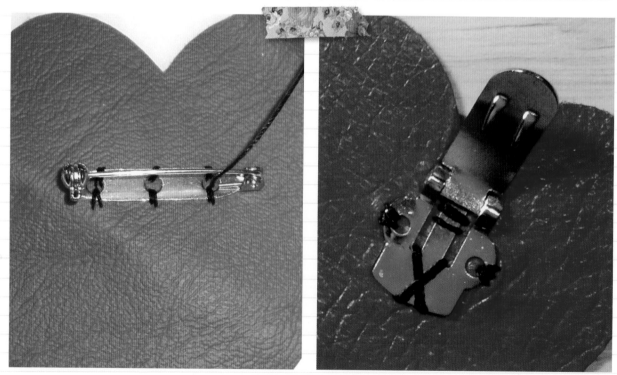

Ring attachments: Ring findings vary, but the one that I have used here has a tiny hole in the middle through which I can pass a needle. On other types of ring attachments, I'd suggest either gluing with a strong epoxy resin or glue gun, or just going crazy with the stitches! Personally I'm more in favour of stitching, as there is far less danger of the ring attachment loosening over time.

Necklace chains: If you use a ready-made necklace chain with the clasp already attached this makes the process simpler. Otherwise, measure the length of chain you want, then attach a clasp to join the ends. To attach the clasp and your leather accessories to your chain, you will need to attach jump rings at the ends using two pairs of flat-nosed pliers: hold each jump ring with one set of pliers, and with the other pair slowly twist the jump ring so that it comes apart at its join, then when you are ready to close the ring, simply twist it back.

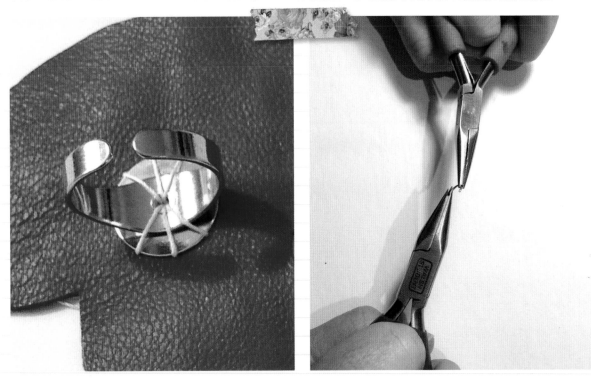

HOW DO I USE THE PROJECT TEMPLATES?

Photocopy the templates, glue the paper copies onto old cereal boxes then carefully cut them out, so they are nice and sturdy to draw around. Before you start drawing around them to cut out the leather or fabric, just make sure you have your templates the right way up. Nearly ten years on, I still position the templates on my leather the wrong way around, which can result in a serious waste of time and leather. In fact, I usually draw a smiley face on my templates to remind me which way up I need to draw around them. I suggest you do the same, and take your time; you want to get it right first time! When drawing around your templates, also remember to check that you are drawing on the suede side of the leather to avoid any slips of the pen that will mark the lovely leather side, which will be the side on show.

WHAT CAN I DO IF I CAN'T SEE MY OUTLINES ON DARK LEATHER?

Sometimes it can be a little bit difficult to see the lines of your templates when you draw on the back of dark leather. First try using a gold pen to see if that helps; if it doesn't, try ironing on some white interfacing instead. Doing this will also stiffen the leather, which can be pretty beneficial if you are cutting out intricate little shapes. Just don't use the iron on a very hot setting, as this can shrink the leather, and that wouldn't be good!

HOW DO I CUT THE INNERS FROM MOUNTBOARD?

To cut out the mountboard inners of flat designs, draw around your finished stitched piece. Then, inside the edge of the shape, draw a smaller version, reducing it by about 5mm (¼in) all the way around. This ensures that when it's all stuck together, sandwiched between two leather layers, your needle will glide happily through the leather without touching the board between. You really don't want to be pushing a needle through all of that!

HOW DO I GLUE MY LEATHER?

You can't pin leather or PVC leatherette, as pins leave holes in the fabric and we don't like that! Instead, use a pva (white) glue or leather cement that dries clear for sticking shapes into place prior to sewing. Let the glue dry once you have it stuck in place, so it doesn't make your needle sticky when you start to sew. You don't need to use loads of this kind of glue, as it is literally used just to hold things in place while you sew. Alternatively, you can use a glue stick, such as Pritt Stick, on larger areas, as this dries quickly and is less messy.

A pva (white) glue or leather cement is also great for when you need to paint a thin line of glue to hold two layers of leather together before you stitch and stuff. Make sure you apply the glue as close to the edge of the leather as possible, otherwise when it comes to stuffing you won't be able to stuff deep into the edges. Try to use only a small amount of glue otherwise it becomes a bit messy; again, it should only be used to secure the leather while you sew. Glue oozing out from the sides while you stitch is not a pretty picture!

HOW DO I STUFF MY LEATHER ACCESSORIES?

A knitting needle comes in handy for poking polyester stuffing into small gaps. Go easy on the stuffing and add it little by little, otherwise you'll be in danger of ending up with a lumpy, overstuffed, unidentifiable object!

TEMPLATES

All of the templates are provided at actual size, so there is no need to enlarge or shrink them for your projects, unless you are free-styling and plan to make a gigantic or teeny-weeny version! Please don't cut up the book, but instead use some tracing paper to copy the templates, or simply photocopy them at 100 per cent unless otherwise instructed.

JANUARY

BOBBLE HAT AND MITTENS TEMPLATES

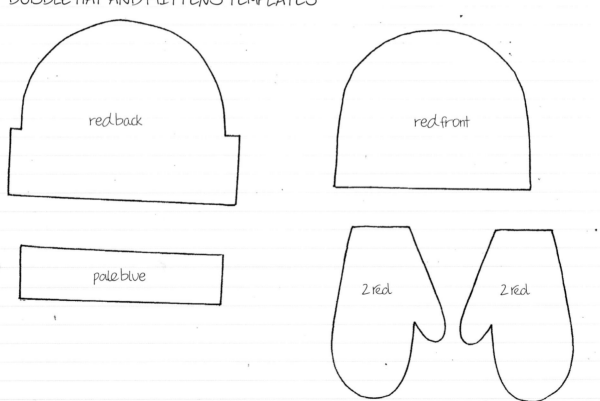

red back

red front

pale blue

2 red   2 red

FEBRUARY

MR AND MRS LOVEHEART TEMPLATES

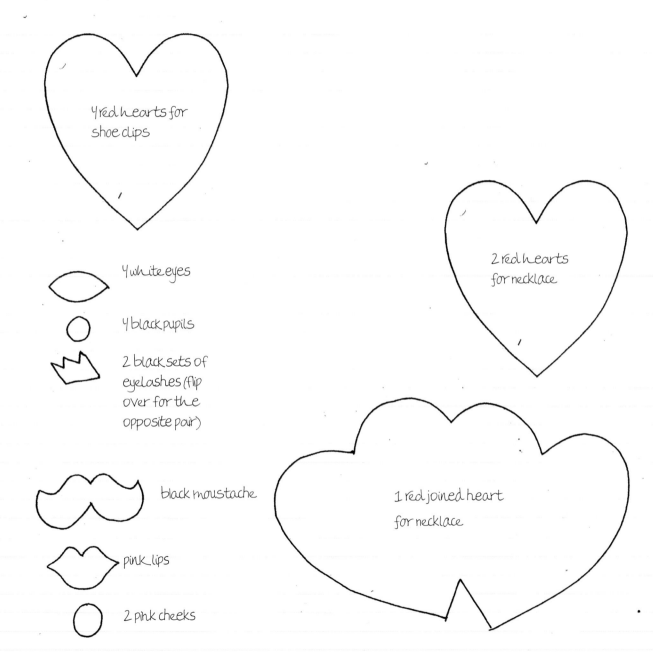

4 red hearts for
shoe clips

4 white eyes

4 black pupils

2 black sets of
eyelashes (flip
over for the
opposite pair)

black moustache

pink lips

2 pink cheeks

2 red hearts
for necklace

1 red joined heart
for necklace

MARCH

BLUE TIT TEMPLATES

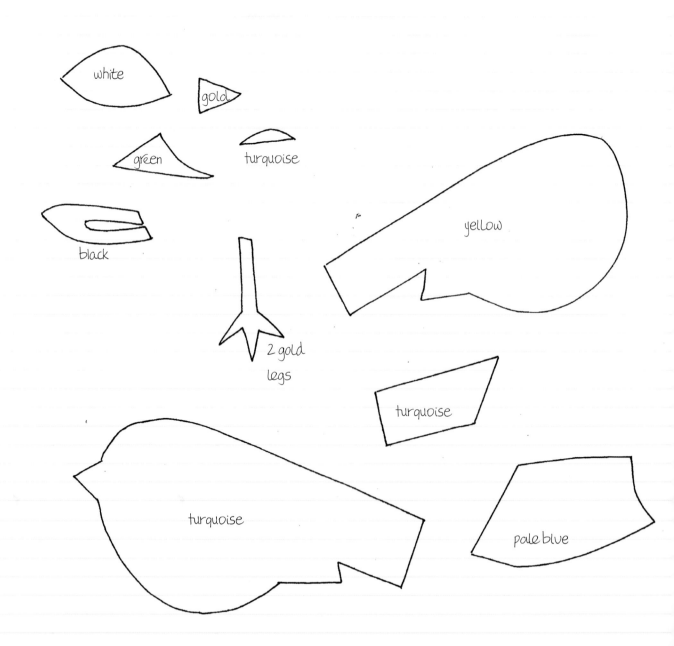

white

gold

green

turquoise

black

yellow

2 gold legs

turquoise

turquoise

pale blue

APRIL

DIPPY EGG TEMPLATES

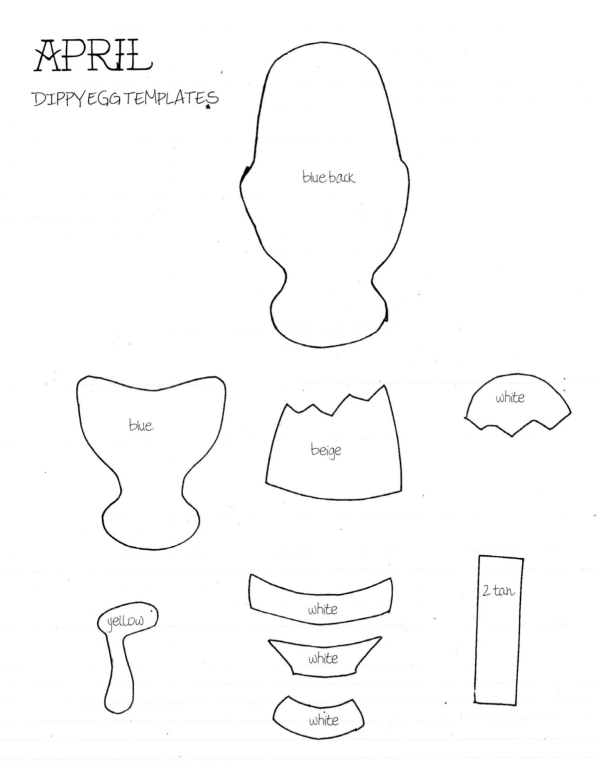

blue back

blue

beige

white

yellow

white

white

white

2 tan

MAY

BUNNY TEMPLATES

back piece

front piece

white

2 pink

pink

pale pink linining

green

pale blue

JUNE

MOUSE TEMPLATES

STRAWBERRY TEMPLATES

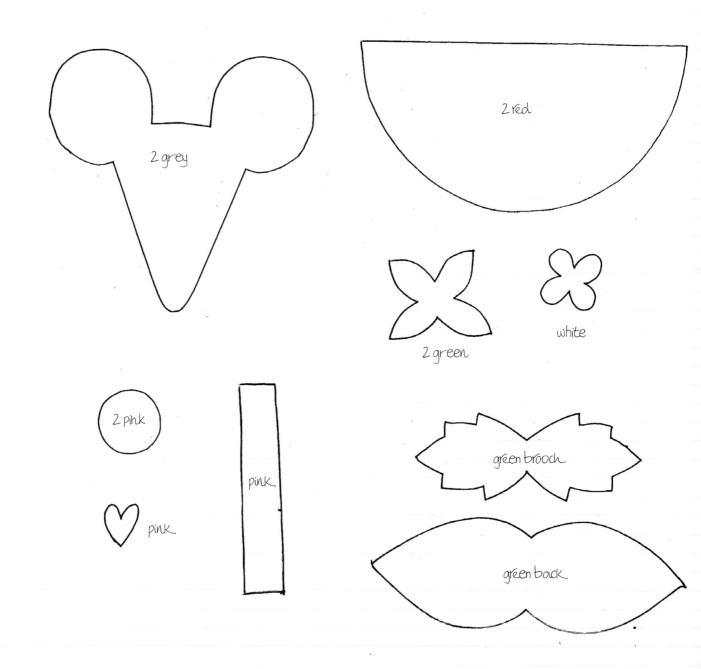

2 grey

2 red

2 green

white

2 pink

pink

pink

green brooch

green back

JULY

MR WHIPPY TEMPLATES

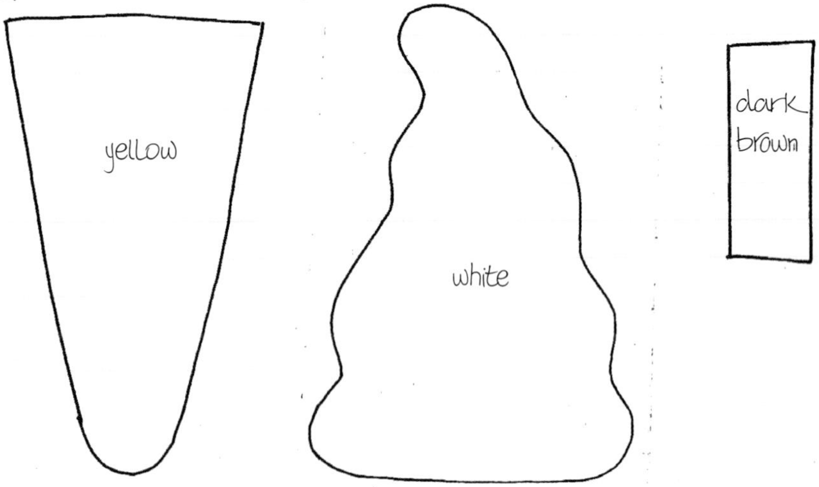

yellow

white

dark brown

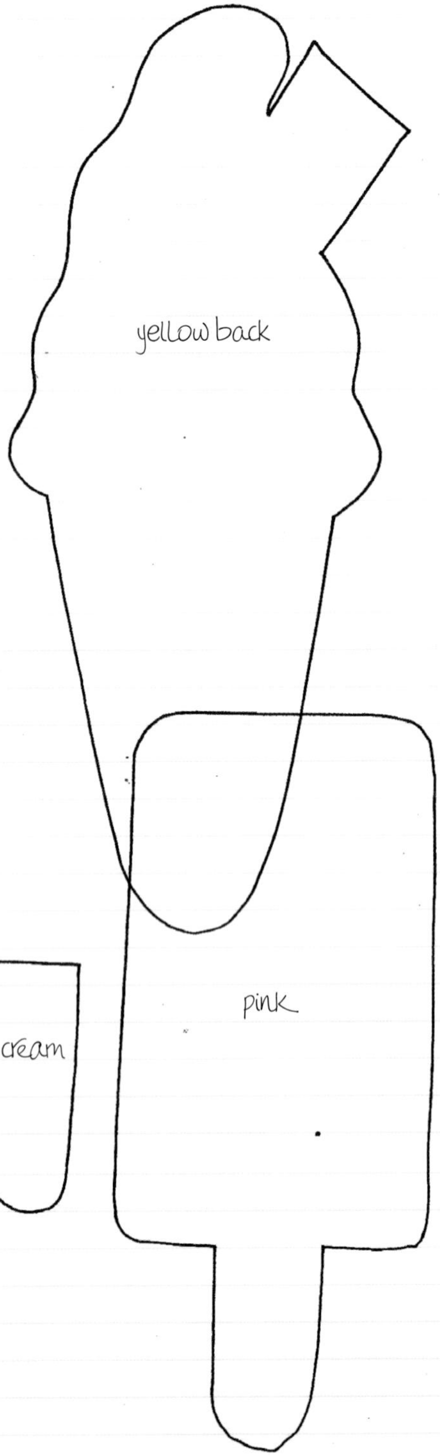

yellow back

FAB LOLLY TEMPLATES

white

dark brown

pink

cream

pink

AUGUST
WATERMELON TEMPLATES

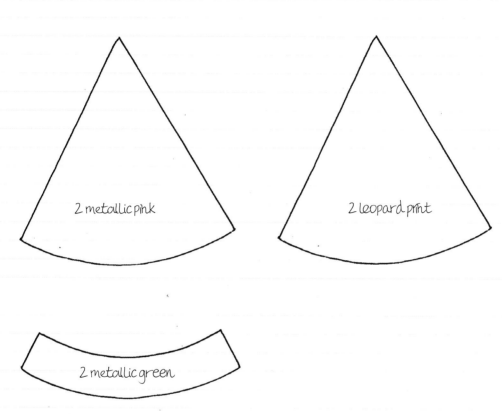

2 metallic pink

2 leopard print

2 metallic green

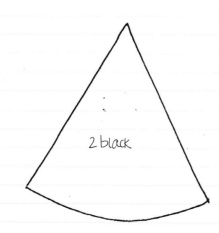

2 black

SEPTEMBER

SUPER SHINY ACORN TEMPLATES

metallic
green

2 gold

2 brown

fold fabric here

collar
shown at 90%
– photocopy at
110%

squirrel
2 orange

2 white

2 pale blue

4 green

flip template
over to cut
the opposite

SQUIRREL TEMPLATES

OCTOBER

TOADSTOOL TEMPLATES

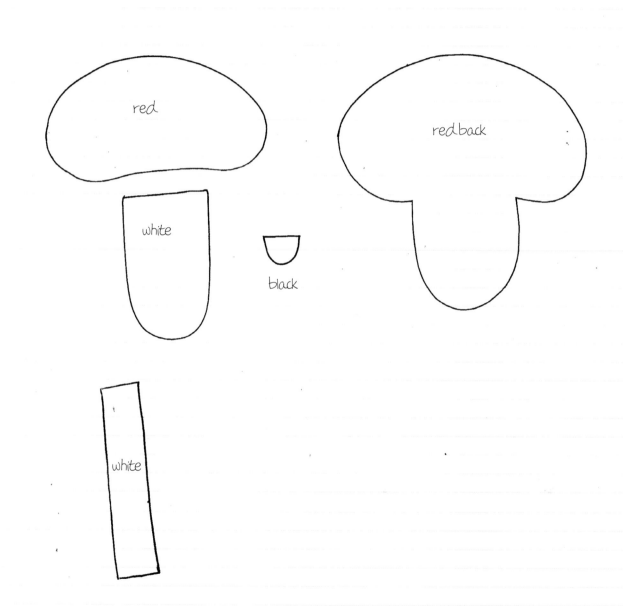

NOVEMBER

ROCKIN' ROBIN TEMPLATES

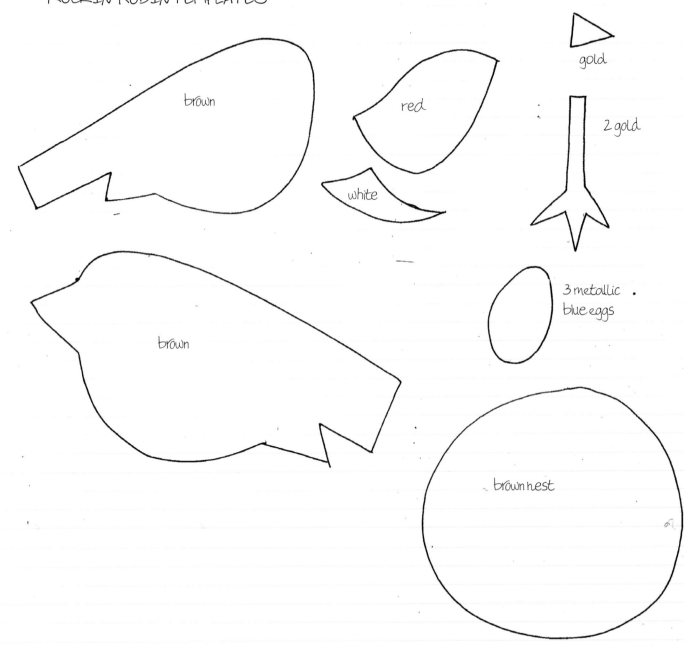

brown

red

white

gold

2 gold

3 metallic blue eggs

brown

brown nest

DECEMBER

CHRISTMAS PUDDING TEMPLATES

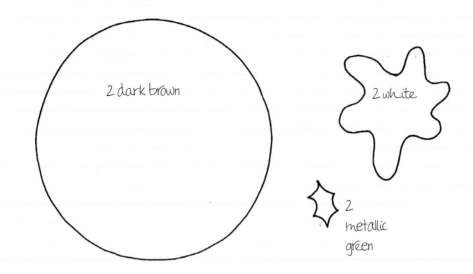

2 dark brown

2 white

2 metallic green

MISTLETOE KISS-MASS TEMPLATES

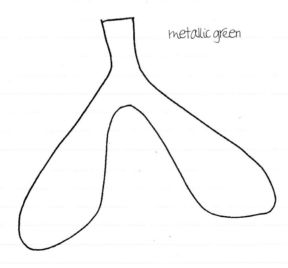

metallic green

SUPPLIERS

Most of the materials and equipment used in this book can be bought from your local craft and haberdashery stores, or you might already have some of the items in your crafty stash. In any case, here's a list of places where you can get the goodies you need to complete the projects.

FINDINGS

From brooch (pin) backs and chains to key rings and jump rings, Creative Beadcraft is the place to head if at all possible. Their London store is a feast for the eyeballs. The more you buy, the cheaper the price, so it's a good place to stock up on findings.

Creative Beadcraft
1 Marshall Street
London
W1F 9BA
www.creativebeadcraft.co.uk

For crafters located further afield, Factory Direct Craft should satisfy all your jewellery finding needs!

Factory Direct Craft
www.factorydirectcraft.com

NEEDLES, THREAD AND OTHER SEWING PARAPHERNALIA

William Gee is an absolute treasure trove of dressmaking supplies. I used to pop into their old fashioned Dalston store when I lived in East London; both the East End staff and fashion designer customers never failed to fascinate me, along with the vast array of sewing stuff neatly displayed behind the counter. Purchase your scissors, topstitch thread and leather needles here or from their website.

William Gee
520-522 Kingsland Road
London
E8 4AR
www.williamgee.co.uk

If a visit to William Gee is not an option try Colonial Needle, which is a great US website where you can find a needle for every job. The site also sells rather a super selection of thimbles!

Colonial Needle
www.colonialneedle.com

And if you're looking for thread in the US or further afield, head to GoldStarTool.

GoldStarTool
goldstartool.com

LEATHER

Finding a leather supplier local to you may prove tricky, unless you live in a large town or city. If you're in London, take a wander around Brick Lane and Bethnal Green Road to discover the leatherwear stores, many of which will sell you small quantities of leather. Otherwise I sell small packs of leather on my website, which will get you started off with the projects in this book.

Love from Hetty and Dave
www.lovefromhettyanddave.co.uk

For readers elsewhere Ebay and Etsy are good online sources, and are easy to buy from in terms of their 'click and buy' facility.

Ebay
www.ebay.com

Etsy
www.etsy.com

Alternativey type 'nappa leather' into your search engine and this will throw up all sorts of results, some of which may be local to you. Sometimes you can purchase job lots of leather offcuts online, which is a great way to build up your stash with various colours.

PVC LEATHERETTE

Your local upholstery store should stock a good selection of faux leather vinyl, which is a suitable substitute for the leather

crafts in this book. Alternatively, try Ebay and Etsy, typing 'faux leather vinyl' into the search engine. Dressmaking PVC is too flimsy for these projects, so always opt for a thick version.

Cloth House on Berwick Street in London does a fabulous range of metallic faux leather PVC, and is always good for a nosy round. Just be aware it is impossble not to spend a fortune in this store if you are a fabric junkie like myself!

Cloth House
47 Berwick St
London
W1F 8SJ

My local upholsterery store, Zebedee Fabrics, is fabulous when it comes to supplying vinyl, and all the lovely staff there are always up for a chit chat.

Zebedee Fabrics
20-126 Seabourne Rd
Bournemouth
BH5 2HY

You could also check out Fabric.com for international suppliers of vinyl who

stock a brilliant selection of colours at reasonable prices.

Fabric.com
www.fabric.com

GENERAL CRAFT SUPPLIES

Other rather brilliant craft stores, or general stores with splendid craft departments include:

Stuff4Crafts
www.stuff4crafts.com

Hobby Lobby
www.hobbylobby.com

The Range
www.therange.co.uk

Hobbycraft
www.hobbycraft.com

Wilko
www.wilko.com

Bargain basement stores that you can find on most high streets are always worth a look for crafty supplies, and usually sell white glue at a super low price.

ABOUT THE AUTHOR

Zoe Larkins is the inspired designer and maker behind the covetable handstitched leather jewellery and accessories label Love from Hetty and Dave.

A graduate of Silversmithing from Kent Institute of Art & Design in 2001, Zoe was soon drawn to the more tactile qualities of leather and textiles, and the possibilities these presented to create original and eclectic designs.

By 2004, inspired by South American folk art, vintage design and 1950s kitsch, Zoe had begun making her own range of handstitched nappa leather handbags, purses, brooches and necklaces, successfully selling them in London's Portobello and Spitalfields markets and establishing a cult following.

Now selling from the website and select boutiques throughout the UK, Europe and Japan, Love from Hetty and Dave designs have been picked up by customers all over the world, including celebrities Amy Winehouse, Deborah 'Dragon' Meaden and Jodie Harsh.

Zoe's highly original best-selling items include upcycled classic 1960s handbags, customized with handsewn decorative leather designs including British birds and animals for a contemporary edge; kooky draught-excluder slug characters; and limited edition, customized shoes comprizing fun animal faces and juicy fruits.

When Zoe isn't sewing, she teaches others to sew at workshops run from her Bournemouth studio. And when she's not doing that, she's baking cakes, lounging around with her cat Jack…oh, and thinking about sewing.

INDEX

A DAVID & CHARLES BOOK
© F&W Media International, Ltd 2014

David & Charles is an imprint of F&W Media International, Ltd
Brunel House, Forde Close, Newton Abbot, TQ12 4PU, UK

F&W Media International, Ltd is a subsidiary of F+W Media, Inc
10151 Carver Road, Suite #200, Blue Ash, OH 45242, USA

Text and Designs © Zoe Larkins
Layout and Photography © F&W Media International, Ltd 2014

First published in the UK and USA in 2014

A catalogue record for this book is available from the British Library.

ISBN-13: 978-1-4463-0479-2 paperback
ISBN-10: 1-4463-0479-5 paperback

Printed in China by RR Donnelley for:
F&W Media International, Ltd
Brunel House, Forde Close, Newton Abbot, TQ12 4PU, UK

10 9 8 7 6 5 4 3 2 1

Acquisitions Editor: Sarah Callard
Desk Editor: Matthew Hutchings
Project Editor: Freya Dangerfield
Design Manager: Sarah Clark
Photographer: Jack Kirby
Production Controller: Kelly Smith

F+W Media publishes high quality books on a wide range of subjects.
For more great book ideas visit: www.stitchcraftcreate.co.uk